THE
FREEZER COOKING MANUAL

FROM
30 DAY GOURMET

A MONTH OF MEALS MADE EASY

Advance Publishing

Indiana

Advance
Publishing

110 Main Street, Advance, Indiana 46102

Cover photography by Jay Tobias
Cover photo kitchen courtesy of Advance Christian Church
Editorial Assistance by Barbara North

Library of Congress Catalog Card Number: 98-93197

Wohlenhaus, Tara and Slagle, Nanci
        The Freezer Cooking Manual from 30 Day Gourmet: A Month of Meals Made Easy /
        Tara Wohlenhaus and Nanci Slagle. – Advance, IN: Advance Publishing, c1998.

        ISBN: 0-9664467-0-4
        1. Cookery   2. Title

Printed in the United States of America

CONTENTS

Dear Friend in the kitchen,

Congratulations on your decision to try (at least once more!!) to organize your cooking. Only those of us who have sung the,

> It's 5 p.m.
> and time to fix dinner
> whatever it is
> I doubt it's a winner☹

blues know the stress created by this one little "task". We know how you feel. Both of us remember the guilt of a supper schedule that read like this:

Sunday:	leftovers
Monday:	taco drive-thru
Tuesday:	tuna sandwiches & chips
Wednesday:	ground beef "helper"
Thursday:	eggs and sausage links
Friday:	pizza pizza
Saturday:	hot dogs/macaroni & cheese

You're not alone! Research now tells us that "most" families in America only eat one "home-cooked" meal a week. Then why do we feel guilty? Because deep down, beyond the busy schedules and ever-present fatigue, most people have similar desires for our evening meal:

1. We want to be together with people we love.
2. We want our food to be nutritious and well-liked.
3. We want to spend our money wisely.

❖❖THE 30 DAY GOURMET COOKING PLAN COULD CHANGE YOUR LIFE!!❖❖

Next week your dinner menus could look something like this:

Sunday:	Beef stroganoff/Champagne salad
Monday:	Broiled pork chops/Mexicali casserole
Tuesday:	Meatloaf/Crispy, cheesy potatoes/quick cobbler
Wednesday:	Parsley parmesan chicken/Pasta with veggies
Thursday:	Baked fish fillets/Wild rice dressing
Friday:	Swiss steak/Make ahead mashed potatoes
Saturday:	Grilled chicken/California pilaf/Fruit slush

Each of these meals took us less than 15 minutes to prepare, plus cooking time. (Except Sunday, of course, when Dad cooks!) We spent no more than $5.00 per entree and we usually have lots of leftovers!
Instead of spendy snacks and fast food lunches we also pulled these from our freezers this week:

chicken fingers	**mozzarella stix**
healthy no-bake cookies	**good-for-you granola bars**

IS THIS SOUNDING GOOD?

Our Goal: The primary focus of this manual is to aid you in preparing a month's worth of dinner entrees for the freezer in one day. For most people, the entree seems to be the problem. If we can gain control of this part, then we can usually come up with side dishes, fruits and vegetables to round out the meal.

We personally assemble about three months' worth of dinner entrees using our plan. Even if you can start with just one week's worth, enough to get you through the "busy season", food to help a family member with special dietary needs, or vacation dinner to thaw and cook in the condo, this book could be your answer.

Cooking the 30 DAY GOURMET way really is worth whatever it takes to make it work for you. Since the summer of 1993 when we began cooking together, we have learned ALOT. We have made all the mistakes (2 gallons of burned white sauce, missed ingredients, recipes that didn't get doubled correctly) and dealt with most of the usual and unusual interruptions (husbands "popping in" for lunch, 1-7 kids underfoot, broken answering machines, crying babies, door-to-door salesmen, and emergency trips to the hospital.)

This manual will help you avoid many of these problems. But, of course, even if you do make mistakes and deal with interruptions, remember - it's worth it!! Nothing beats the relief and great sense of accomplishment we feel when we can take an entree out of the freezer in the morning, go to the zoo (or to our office!) for the day, and come home to a 10 minute prep time for dinner.

❖

This is a hands-on manual. Make copies of the worksheet pages as you'll use these each month. Having everything in one book is SO helpful. We have wasted a lot of valuable time looking for recipes, searching for last month's ingredient list, and rewriting the same worksheets each time. We are so glad to have this organized manual for ourselves, too!

❖

Have fun! And please don't think of 30 DAY GOURMET as another one of those great ideas thought up by superhuman, nearly perfect 90's women. We are just a couple of average moms. Our kids' baby books are only half-filled, our closets are a mess, and only one of us is a great cook by nature. As our pastor frequently says, "We are all fellow strugglers". This is just one little corner of our lives that we have finally organized and boy does it feel great! So, give our system a try and see what happens. It has helped thousands of frustrated cooks who felt forever doomed to drive-thru windows. We're guessing that it just may change your life, too!   Happy (infrequent) cooking - and please let us know how it goes.

With our warm (fresh out-of-the-oven) wishes,

Nanci Slagle

Tara Wohlenhaus

TOP TEN REASONS TO TRY THE 30 DAY GOURMET PLAN

1. You will love the convenience.

The **30 DAY GOURMET** plan makes the whole day so much easier. Just take something out of the freezer in the morning and then don't give it another thought until late afternoon. It's great!

2. You will save $$$$$$.

We all know that eating out or buying today for tonight's dinner can be very costly. Most families of 5 spend at least $15-$20 on a fast food dinner or pre-packaged frozen dinners. The **30 DAY GOURMET** plan is guaranteed to lower your food bills! We spend no more than $4.00-$5.00 for each dinner entree that we prepare for our families. Think of what you could save! And when we do eat out, the kids are thrilled and appreciative!

3. You will have enough to share with others.

Charity and hospitality seem to be lost arts today. By assembling your food in advance, it's easy to take dinner to the neighbor who is ill, your friend who just had a baby, or the family that recently moved in across the street. By cooking multiples of the same recipe, it's also easy to take another entree out of the freezer for company, even unexpected guests.

4. Your health will improve.

You will eat fewer processed foods, fats, salt, and preservatives because you are in control of each recipe.

5. You will enjoy fresh, home-cooked taste.

You will eat less "cardboard box" and fewer "drive-thru" meals. Will you miss them?

6. You will enjoy a greater variety of foods.

You do not have to eat the same foods seven days a week. You can be as exotic or ordinary as you please. We now enjoy opening the freezer door and making choices between food from several national origins.

7. You will enjoy more time with your family.

By planning your meals in advance, you can enjoy the after school hours and the after dinner hours with your children, spouse, or friends. Clean up is drastically reduced. You will have less pots and pans and large cookware to wash.

8. You will have less stress between 4-6 p.m.

In most households, this time slot is the most hectic of the day. Dinner prep time will be much more relaxed due to your careful planning.

9. You will prepare your own fast foods.

Sandwich fillings, hamburger patties, spaghetti sauce, chicken nuggets, etc. . . are great for those especially hectic times when you need dinner QUICK!

10. You will have a happier family.

No more *"go away and play while I slave over a hot stove"* or *"Go somewhere? - who's going to clean up this mess?"*

TOP TEN EXCUSES FOR NOT TRYING THE 30 DAY GOURMET PLAN

1. **My Schedule is too busy now. I could never take a whole day just to cook.**

   After you try the 30 DAY GOURMET plan, you will realize that the time you save in meal preparation and cleanup each evening is well worth the time it takes to shop and cook in bulk.

2. **I don't have a freezer.**

   Neither did Nanci when we started. Actually, a month's worth of main dish entrees WILL fit into a standard refrigerator's freezer. But it does help to have some extra space. We would suggest asking around, shopping the garage sales and auctions, or sharing space with a neighbor. A full freezer works much more efficiently than a half empty one.

3. **I HATE casseroles.**

   30 DAY GOURMET cooking doesn't mean you have to eat casseroles every night. It means you prepare and freeze the foods you know your family likes. Some cooks might only make pizzas, hamburger patties, and baked chicken. Others enjoy combined foods and may make more casseroles.

4. **I could never come up with the money to get started.**

   Of course, you realize that you WILL be spending the money eventually. Try stocking up on grocery items as you see great sales. After a month or two, you should have most of the ingredients. Have a garage sale, use your Christmas bonus, or earmark that tax return check for some quick cash. Or try just cooking for 2 weeks the first time.

5. **I don't have enough pans or containers to hold all the food.**

   No problem. Use freezer ziptop bags. They can be thawed and put into your favorite dish for baking. Slowly acquire freezer containers, glass casseroles, and metal baking pans at garage sales and discount stores.

6. **I hate to cook!**

   But you have to eat, right? Then isn't it best to do most of your cooking ONCE every 4-6 weeks and get it over with?

7. **I would miss fresh baked/cooked foods.**

   Having 30 main dish entrees in the freezer just gives you the flexibility to decide WHEN you want to cook or bake "from scratch". We seem to have more energy now for creative side dishes, desserts, and bigger company meals. Our entrees are made "from scratch". Most entrees are NOT pre-baked just pre-assembled and frozen. All the aromas and flavors of fresh remain.

8. **I'm not disciplined enough to do it.**

   We're not either! Having a cooking partner really helps keep us accountable. And once you do this a few times, you won't want to go back to the "old ways". If you cook alone, you just have to set the date and stick to it NO MATTER WHAT!

9. **I have no idea what freezes successfully.**

   Keep reading the planner and we'll tell you! Actually, more things freeze well than don't.

10. **I enjoy cooking every night!**

   That's great! Open a restaurant and we'll come for a visit☺.

7 STEPS TO THE 30 DAY GOURMET PLAN

1. SET A TIME TO PLAN

2. TAKE INVENTORY

3. HAVE YOUR PLANNING SESSION

    ❖ Choose Your Recipes
    ❖ Convert Your Recipes
    ❖ Plan Your Freezing Containers
    ❖ Plan Your Shopping
    ❖ Divide and Conquer

4. GO SHOPPING

5. PREPARE FOR ASSEMBLY DAY

6. ASSEMBLE ENTREES & STOCK FREEZER

7. CLEAN UP & EVALUATE

Before you begin:
DECIDE IF YOU WILL COOK ALONE OR WITH A FRIEND

❖ Advantages of cooking with a friend.

1. Share recipes.

This really helps with the rut that all cooks get into-fixing the same things each week. Wouldn't you rather try something you know another family actually eats than a new recipe with 25 ingredients??

2. Share the work.

In the long run, it is really much less time-consuming to cook for two families at once. After all, you are getting out all the same appliances, cookware, and ingredients anyway.

3. Share the fun!

OK, we admit it! This is what keeps us coming back. We really look forward to the 8-hour chat we get to have every time we cook together. It's a great way to get closer to a friend. (If you especially HATE to cook, this part of the plan will really help to take the drudgery out of your meal chores.)

4. Share the thrill!

Although our families are very supportive of our cooking and really enjoy the finished product, they just don't get quite as excited as we do.
Family's response: *"Looks OK to me. What is it? That's nice."*
Cook's responses: *"Wow, don't those meatballs look fantastic? They held together great. Beautiful!"*

5. Share the knowledge and abilities.

In our situation, Tara has a broad range of cooking and nutrition knowledge. Nanci contributes math skills and shopping finesse. When we pool our brains and talent, we really do pretty well and are a lot less afraid to cook than we would be alone.

6. Share the cookware.

One very economical reason for cooking with a partner is that each cook doesn't have to purchase every necessary item. Between the two (or more) of you, you might come up with plenty of pans, utensils, measuring cups, etc. Only one of you needs a food processor or blender, electric can opener, and mixer.

❖ Things to consider when choosing a cooking partner:

1. Sizes of your families.

It helps if you have similar sized families so that you can split everything down the middle. Otherwise, the smaller family will always have lots more meals - which may work out OK too, depending on your lifestyles and eating patterns. Whichever one of us runs out of food first usually buys main entrees from the other so that we still want to cook at the same time. Just hope that you like what she's selling!!☺

2. Your basic tastes.

If you each choose your 10 favorite meals and none of them is the same, you probably shouldn't cook together. Most cooks can usually agree on 8-10 recipes!
Note: We also make allowances all the time for who likes onions, spices, whole wheat pastas, etc.

3. Your compatibility.

Don't just ask the best cook you know to be your **30 DAY GOURMET** cooking partner. A good question to ask yourself is, *"Who would I look forward to spending a whole day with?☺"*

STEP 1
SET A TIME TO PLAN

Whether you are cooking solo or with a friend, you need a few hours to plan. We usually just meet at Tara's farm, turn the kids loose and make a day of it, but it doesn't have to take more than a few hours.

The first time you plan, it will seem to take forever. Going through recipes, thinking of what your family likes, and discussing it all is very time consuming. But you WILL get much quicker!

By all means, DO NOT TRY TO PLAN OVER THE PHONE. Meet at the park, turn a video on for the kids, or even hire a sitter, but PLAN to spend some time. Set an exact date, time and place. Put it on your calendar and don't let anything keep you from it!

*Complete *Worksheet A* and set your day for planning.
*Fill out *Worksheet B* before planning day arrives.
*During Planning Day write in your scheduled Shopping Day & Assembly Day.

Worksheet A
PLANNING DAY WORKSHEET

Planning Day __3/28__   Planning Time __Noon - 3:00__
Where? __Tara's__   Kids' Activities __lunch outside,__
__new video, library books, puzzles, snack table__

What to bring: ☑ 10-15 recipes my family likes
              ☑ *Worksheet B* (inventory list of my ingredients on hand)
              ☑ calendar to decide shopping and cooking days
              ☑ other: __Supermarket ads__
                    __lunch stuff, lemonade__
                    __Kids swimsuits & towels__

Shopping day __4/6__   Assembly Day __4/8__

11

Worksheet B
ON HAND INVENTORY SHEET

*Update this list each month before your planning day and bring it with you.

*We keep certain items in stock just for our cooking. Lots of these are ordered from our food buying club or bought ahead on super sales. We split the cost on all of these items. They might include:

rice	freezer bags	spices
tomato sauce	tomatoes	flour
pasta	mushrooms (canned)	salt
cheeses (frozen)	oil	oatmeal

*These items are all kept in a central location meaning whoever has an extra closet! Again, it helps to keep these at the designated "cooking house".

*We also write down those items that we each might have around that we are willing to contribute to assembly day. Remember, you will save money and space, if you use up what you have first. We "guesstimate" the value of these items.

*One Worksheet B for each cook is best.

ITEMS IN STOCK

	Item Name	Quantity?	Where?	Cost?
1.	Quick brown rice	3 pounds	T's pantry	1.40
2.	Whole peeled tomatoes	3/12 oz. cans	T's pantry	.79 ea
3.	elbow macaroni	8 pounds	T's pantry	5.40
4.	Shredded cheddar cheese	5 pounds	T's freezer	10.50
5.	garlic powder	1/2 pound	T's pantry	3.12
6.	chili powder	1/2 pound	T's pantry	2.75
7.	Sliced mushrooms	4/10 oz. cans	Nanci's	6.30
8.	flour	25 pounds	T's freezer	9.75
9.	whole wheat flour	15 pounds	T's freezer	7.00
10.	milk	2 gallons	N's	4.00
11.	eggs	1 dozen	N's	.75
12.	mayonnaise	32 oz.	N's	2.00
13.	margarine	1 pound	N's	.50
14.	butter	1 pound	T's	1.50
15.				

STEP 3
HAVE YOUR PLANNING SESSION

❖ CHOOSE YOUR RECIPES

❖ **Have each cook bring 5-10 main dish recipes their family likes.**
This gives you a place to begin. Almost anything you like to eat can be at least partially made ahead and frozen.

❖ **It's best to start with a total of just 8-10 recipes.**
If you assemble 3 meals of each recipe, that's 24-30 entrees. We have found that between leftovers, dinners out, and meals from scratch (like pancake suppers), it's plenty of food for 4-5 weeks.
Rule of thumb: The more recipes you use, the longer your assembly day will be.

❖ **Start with tried and true recipes.**
Kids (and spouses) may resist new food night after night, especially if they are used to eating out or having TV dinners. Some ideas:

hamburger patties	sloppy joes
chili	spaghetti sauce
baked chicken	meatloaf
chicken nuggets	chicken patties

❖ **Don't take more than 1 recipe out of a book or magazine.**
Of course, it looks and sounds good. They all do! It's best to test a recipe on your own family once before committing to eating it 3 times a month (plus leftovers).

❖ **Always do at least 1 crock pot meal.**
It cooks by itself overnight or during cooking day and all you do is "bag and admire" it.
Sometimes we do 1 crock pot meal the night before and then do another one on assembly day!

❖ **Consider the season.**
In the summer, we prepare lots of hamburger patties, ribs, and meats in marinade for the grill.
Chili, soup, and stews are winter favorites.

❖ **Be sure that your entree is freezable.**
Some basic rules of freezing are:
1. Don't freeze raw vegetables unless they have been blanched. This includes potatoes. (Refer to the Blanching Chart in the Appendix.) Blanching is a short period of cooking that seals in color, vitamins, texture, and flavor. Purchased, frozen vegetables may be used as they are. They have already been blanched.
2. Large pieces of hard boiled egg may have an unpleasant texture if frozen.
3. Cornstarch sauces and gravies made with flour and oil or butter tend to separate when being reheated after freezing. These sauces are acceptable for freezing when they are mixed with other ingredients. Our Fat Free White Sauce recipe (See Side Dishes/Misc.) freezes very well. It helps to reheat these dishes on lower heat. Do not allow them to boil while reheating.
4. Don't thaw raw meat and re-freeze it without thoroughly cooking it first. When you want to freeze meat in its raw form, it must be fresh from the start.
5. Cured meat, like ham and bacon, should be eaten within 1 month after freezing. These meats develop a strong flavor during long term storage in the freezer.

6. Deep fried foods will not stay crispy after thawing.

7. Egg and milk replacers freeze fine in most recipes.

8. Fully cooked pasta and rice tend to turn mushy when frozen in liquids. We suggest cooking these starches only half the recommended cooking time on the packaging instructions if it will be placed in broth, soups and stews or casseroles.

❖CONVERT YOUR RECIPES (Worksheet C)

❖We suggest converting your own recipes into sizes that will feed your family 1 meal. If an 8-10 serving recipe will give you too many leftovers, cut the recipe in half to serve 4-5.

❖Look at our worksheet C sample on page 11. This measure will surely save you some headaches on assembly day. By multiplying out the ingredients ahead, you save time on assembly day and cut down on mathematical errors. Use our Equivalency Chart in the *Appendix* to help you. Make sure and note any changes you will make from the original recipe on the Assembly Directions section of the card. The primary aim of this conversion process is to determine exactly what can be done to this recipe now, so that you will have as little as possible to do on the day you want to eat this entree.

❖PLAN YOUR FREEZING CONTAINERS

Be sure to mark on your Recipe Card what kind of container you will need to freeze each entree in. Choosing the right containers for your food is important, but not difficult. Here are the main freezing methods we use:

RIGID PLASTIC CONTAINERS

These are very commonly found in supermarkets, discount stores, etc. Some people buy these containers at home parties and some prefer to recycle large margarine tubs, or other containers. We have found these containers to be a good choice if you have a large freezer where they stack very neatly. Plastic containers can be re-used until they crack. Containers manufactured specifically for freezing can be expensive but last much longer. Do not pour very hot or boiling foods into plastic containers. Cool the foods first, and allow adequate headspace (air at the top) for expansion in freezing. About 1/2" at the top of a quart of liquids is plenty. Freezer labels should be applied to your containers, labeled with the date, contents, and any cooking instructions you wish to include. there are some very nice containers which can go from the freezer to microwave to refrigerator. We have found that containers with squared corners use the space in your freezer more efficiently. We have also found that re-cycled margarine or whipped topping tubs can allow too much air to come in contact with the food. If you must use these re-cycled containers, try placing a layer or two of plastic wrap over the surface of the food in the container. If you notice signs of freezer burn on the food, don't reuse that container. Do not reheat foods in the recycled containers. They were not made to resist high temperatures.

FREEZER BAGS

These may be a good choice for homes with limited freezer space. Make sure you purchase bags manufactured for freezing. "Food storage" bags are not heavy enough to ensure good protection for foods in the freezer. Cooled food is placed in the bag, all possible air removed, and sealed. The bags of food can be flattened with the palm of a hand to distribute the food evenly. This flattening allows the bags to be stacked on top of each other in the freezer and allows for quicker freezing. The bags should be labeled before the food is put in them. The label should include the same information as above for rigid plastic containers. Wipe the bags free of any moisture to keep them from sticking together when frozen. Freezer bags may be washed and reused as long as they did not previously contain any raw eggs or meats.

An 8" or 9" pie pan will slide into a gallon size freezer bag, and 9x13 baking pans and many casserole dishes will fit inside a 2 gallon freezer bag. You may wish to place all the separate parts of a recipe into smaller bags, but store them together in a larger bag.

GLASS CONTAINERS

Combined foods such as casseroles may be frozen in the glass dish in which you plan to serve it. When the food in the glass container has cooled sufficiently, wrap it with freezer weight foil, freezer paper, or slide it into a large freezer bag as above. The main advantage of freezing in glass is that you can freeze, defrost, bake, and refrigerate in the same container. This is very convenient and cost effective. Glass containers may be obtained in the usual retail stores but be sure to check out garage sales, second hand stores, and your mother's cabinets and garage.

Recipe: Cheeseburger Quiche

Meals:

Ingredients:	serves 6	1	2	3	4	5	6
Pie shell, unbaked		1	2	3	4	5	6
browned ground beef		2½ C.	5 C.	7½ C.	10 C.	12½ C.	15 C.
mayonnaise		½ C.	1 C.	1½ C.	2 C.	2½ C.	3 C.
milk		½ C.	1 C.	1½ C.	2 C.	2½ C.	3 C.
diced onion		2 T.	¼ C.	¼ C. +2T.	½ C.	½ C. +2T.	¾ C
eggs		2	4	6	8	10	12
cornstarch		1 T.	2 T.	3 T.	4 T.	5 T.	6 T.
shredded cheese		1½ C	3 C.	4½ C.	6 C.	7½ C.	9 C.

Containers: quiche pans or pie pans, freezer bags or foil to wrap.

Assembly Directions:
In mixing bowl blend mayonnaise, milk, eggs and cornstarch. Distribute beef, onion, and cheese into pie shells or into freezer bags. Pour egg mixture into pie shells or into the freezer bags.

Freezing and Cooking Directions:
To pre-bake before freezing - preheat oven to 350°. Bake 35-40 minutes or until a knife inserted in the center comes out wet, but clean. Cool, then wrap and freeze. To freeze mixture in bags - keep shells on hand. Seal quiche filling in freezer bag and freeze.
To serve pre-baked quiche- thaw, then warm in a 300° oven for 20 min.
If frozen in bag, thaw mixture, pour into shell, then bake in a preheated oven 35-40 minutes.

Comments: Purchase or home-made shells ok. fat free or reg. mayo or salad dressing works. Sausage, ham, or bacon sub. for burger. Cheddar or swiss cheese best. Cheese can be cut by ⅓ to save on fats.

STEP 3
HAVE YOUR PLANNING SESSION

❖ PLAN YOUR SHOPPING

  ❖ **Fill out the Tally Sheet - *(Worksheet E)***

Use the sample tally sheet below as a guide.

Finalize your entrees for the month and write them in the left hand column of *Worksheet E*.

Follow the directions on the cover of the blank Tally Sheet found in the *Worksheets Section* to fill out the form. This form will give you a complete list of all ingredients and other essentials you will need on Assembly Day.

Recipe Title	Meals For Cook #1	Meals For Cook #2	Ground Beef, Fresh	Ground Beef Frozen	Boneless Breast	Chicken Parts	Cooked Diced	Whole Turkey	Ground Turkey	Turkey Breast	Cooked Diced	Ground Pork	Ham	Pork Sausage	Bacon	Frozen Fillets	Fresh Fillets	Eggs	Margarine	Butter	Sour Cream	White Sauce	Grated Parmesan	Grated Cheddar
Food Type / Beef / Chicken / Turkey / Pork / Seafood / Dairy																								
1. Crispy Rice Chicken	2	2			12#													4						
2. Turkey Tetrazzini	1	2					12c															18c	3c	
3. Chicken Divan	2	1	24																			9c		3c
4.																								
5.																								
6.																								
7.																								
8.																								
9.																								
10.																								
11.																								
12.																								
Total Needed			24	12			12c															27	3	3
− Total on Hand			0	10			12c															0	3	3
= Total to Buy			24	2			0															27	0	0

Recipe Title	Meals For Cook #1	Meals For Cook #2	Rice Cereal Crumbs	Broken Spaghetti	Rice cooked			Mushrooms	Broccoli Spears		Green Pepper		Flour	Oil	Ketchup
Food Type / Grains, Pasta, Dry Beans, Breads, Crumb Crackers / Frozen Produce / Fresh Produce															
1. Crispy Rice Chicken	2	2	6c												
2. Turkey Tetrazzini	1	2		24c				24a			1½				
3. Chicken Divan	2	1			9c				3¾a						
4.															
5.															
6.															
7.															
8.															
9.															
10.															
11.															
12.															
Total Needed			6c	24	9			24	3¾		1½				
− Total on Hand			0	24	4			10	2		0				
= Total to Buy			6c	0	5			14	1¾		1½				

STEP 3
HAVE YOUR PLANNING SESSION

❖ Fill out the Shopping List (*Worksheet E*)

Transfer the ingredients and numbers from the "Total Needed" column on the Tally Sheet (*Worksheet D*) to the appropriate columns on your Shopping List (*Worksheet E*).

❖ Tips to Plan Your Shopping:

1. Write in the total pounds, ounces, cups, etc. of each item. For example, canned, whole tomatoes are sold by the ounce. Rather than writing *"6- 28 oz. cans"* write *"canned tomatoes - 168 oz."* By doing this, you might see that you can buy one food service size can, meaning less time with the can opener.
2. Use the Equivalency Chart found in the *Appendix* to assist you in tallying items.
3. In the miscellaneous column, include such things as freezer bags, foil, freezer tape, freezer labels, rubber gloves, trash bags, permanent markers, dish soap, and snacks and lunch for Assembly Day. (We usually buy ourselves and the kids a treat or two!)
4. Check your grocery advertisements and decide where to get what. It really pays to shop around, especially when buying large quantities. In our area, at least one of the chain stores is usually running chicken and beef on sale.
5. You may use a different shopping list for each store you will visit, or use one list and highlight each store's specials with a different color.
6. Check to see if there is a food buying club or cooperative in your area. A Cooperative is a warehouse that will take orders for bulk and retail pack foods and sell them at wholesale prices. We save TONS of money this way. For more information, see the Food Cooperative Information Sheet in the *Appendix*.
7. When you know what quantities you will need, call the supermarket meat counter well in advance and ask about quantity discounts and bulk packaging.
8. The meat department will also grind special meats for you, mix different ground meats together thoroughly, slice large cuts, cube steaks and many other helpful things. Just ask early enough to give them adequate time to fill your order.
9. Buy jars of chopped/minced garlic in the produce section of your grocery store. This will save a lot of "clove crushing".

Worksheet E Sample
SHOPPING LIST

Beef	Canned Foods	Frozen Produce	Spices
fresh ground	Tomato Sce.	broccoli cuts	garlic powder
7 pounds	132 oz.	2 pounds	2 oz
Stew beef	Tomato paste	carrots	cumin
6 pounds	8 oz.	1 pound	2 oz
Chuck roast	Kidney beans	Peas	black pepper

STEP 3
HAVE YOUR PLANNING SESSION

❖ DIVIDE AND CONQUER
    ❖ Fill out the "What To Do Before Assembly Day" list (*Worksheet F*).
Use the sample page below to help you decide who will need to complete what tasks before Assembly Day arrives.

Worksheet F Sample
WHAT TO DO BEFORE ASSEMBLY DAY

*Fill out this sheet during your planning session. You will need one for each cook.

Cook #1 __Tara__

1. brown beef
2. steam onions/celery
3. dice ham
4. grind ham
5. cook beans

Cook #2 __Nanci__

1. white sauce
2. cook pasta
3. skin chicken parts
4. shred swiss cheese
5. shred carrots

---

*Before your planning session ends, decide who will bring what items to the kitchen where Assembly Day will take place. Remember, just one missing item could cost you a few hours☺.

Worksheet F Sample
WHAT TO BRING ON ASSEMBLY DAY

*Include your "On Hand Inventory" items needed as well as appliances, pots, bowls, and containers for your meals.

Cook #1 __Tara__

1. lg. cookware
2. long handle utensils
3. inventory foods
4. freezer bags
5. foil

Cook #2 __Nanci__

1. large measuring cups
2. cutting boards
3. prep work foods
4. inventory foods
5. food processor

STEP 4
GO SHOPPING

❖ **Before you go. . .**

☑ Clean out your refrigerator and freezer. You will need as much room as possible for the many groceries that you will bring home.

☑ Be sure you have enough time to get the job done. It's much easier to do it all at once than to run out 4 different times.

❖ **When to go. . .**

☑ Although we stock up non-perishable items all month long, the perishable groceries and meats that you want to start with fresh should be purchased no more than 2 days before Assembly Day.

☑ Be sure to leave yourself enough time to get your prep work done. If you make the mistake (like we have) of not shopping until the evening before Assembly Day, then you end up being on your feet for what seems like 3 days straight!

❖ **What to take. . .**

☑ Wear comfortable clothing and supportive shoes.

☑ Take along the following items:

☑ Tally Sheet (Worksheet D)	☑ Calculator
☑ Shopping List (Worksheet E)	☑ Equivalency Chart
☑ Cooler (in summer)	☑ Store Advertisements
☑ Adequate cash/checks	☑ Extra bags or boxes
☑ Lunch/snacks	☑ Water/juice to drink
☑ Gas in your vehicle	☑ Pain Relievers☺

What to leave at home:

☑ children	☑ pets

Usually, one of us shops while the other one takes care of all the children.
Each of us thinks she got the better end of the deal!

❖ **More Tips:**

1. Try buying your large quantity items in bulk. Check out restaurant supply stores and discount warehouses. This will save you money and lots of the time it takes storing, opening, using, and throwing away many small cans or jars.

2. Look for freezer labels near the freezer containers and freezer wrap.

3. Try to bag your groceries as you buy them according to where they will need to stay that day. You have already decided who will do what tasks, so try to keep the items for each cook separated. Extra bags and cardboard boxes already in your vehicle are handy for this.

4. Be sure that you have plenty of dish soap for Assembly Day. Things could come to a screeching halt rather quickly without it!

5. Grocers will often waive the "Limits" advertised on specials (especially meat) if you order large quantities 3-4 days before you need them.

6. Sometimes the little grocer is the best person to deal with. He REALLY wants your business and will help you out all he can. We raised quite a commotion recently when we went into Tara's small town grocery and bought 240 chicken breasts, 6 turkey breasts, and 30 lbs. of ground beef!

STEP 5
PREPARE FOR ASSEMBLY DAY

❖ We try to think of it as a "cooking week". Of course, it doesn't take a whole week, but there are things that HAVE to be done ahead if this is going to work. Just remember:
YOU ONLY DO THIS EVERY 4-6 WEEKS
IT WILL BE WORTH IT!!!!!!

❖ We think of the week in 4 processes:

    ❖Planning   ❖Shopping   ❖Divide and Conquer   ❖Assembly Day
❖ We've already covered the first 2 processes, so you are half way done!

Our rule for *Divide and Conquer* is:
THE MORE WE GET DONE BEFORE ASSEMBLY DAY, THE BETTER!

❖ We try to divide these pre-Assembly Day chores between us:

skin chicken parts	*soak beans*
brown ground beef	*cook pasta*
dice or grind ham	*make bread/cracker crumbs*
make white sauce	*start crock pot meal*
cook and dice chicken/turkey	*chop/shred vegetables*

❖ To be honest, some Assembly Days we have started with NONE of these things done. It made for a much longer Assembly Day, but it was better than not cooking at all.

❖ It also helps to explain what you are about to embark on to your family and friends. They need to know that this will require a big time commitment from you, but that the results will be worth it. Go over your cooking week schedule with them and ask them to help you. For us that usually means:

    1. *Help to carry in groceries*
    2. *Someone to watch the baby while the hot turkey is diced*
    3. *Help with meal preparations while you do other important tasks*
       to get ready for Assembly Day. (It's OK to send them OUT!)

❖ If you are traveling to your cooking partner's house:
    1. Put as much "stuff" in your vehicle the night before as possible.
    2. Post your copy of *Worksheet F* on the fridge and check it frequently.
    3. Turn your freezer to its coldest temperature in preparation for the foods you will bring home.
❖ If you are hosting the Assembly Day:
    1. Clean off your countertops and create more table space.
    2. Empty your trash and set out a LARGE can.
    3. Set out your mixing bowls/pans/utensils,etc.
    4. Turn your freezer to its coldest temperature.

STEP 6
ASSEMBLE ENTREES & STOCK FREEZER

THE BIG DAY HAS FINALLY ARRIVED!
Here is a list of items you will find useful for Assembly Day:

Long handled utensils, including:
forks	slotted spoons
ladles	wire whisks
tongs	metal/rubber spatulas

Large containers for mixing, including:
- dish pans
- mixing bowls
- water bath canners

Other items:

large, rimmed baking sheets	9x13 baking pans
microwaveable containers	large skillets with lids
heat-proof pads/pot holders	mixing bowls with handles and pour spouts
oven mitts	extra kitchen timers
electric hand mixer	large containers with lids for marinating/chilling
electric stand mixer	large sized sets of measuring cups
electric can opener	standard measuring cup sets
electric skillets/hot plates	standard measuring spoon sets
food processor or blender	cookie/ice cream scoops (for forming meatballs)
several sizes of sharp knives	large colanders and strainers
crock pots	large electric roasting pans

❖Assembly Day Procedures

We try hard to start by 9 a.m. and are usually still washing dishes in the evening. On the IDEAL Assembly Day, we have no kids to watch, no lunch to fix, and nowhere to be that night. Our husbands take the kids out to dinner and then bring them home and put them to bed. Then they rub our feet and say, *"Honey, why don't you go soak in the tub while I finish cleaning up."* On REAL Assembly Days, we sometimes have 1 sick kid, nothing for lunch, and three evening meetings we are expected to attend. We just don't want you to get frustrated striving for perfection. No one has the perfect cooking partner, mate, kids, or schedule. Be flexible. You'll live longer!

1. **Decide where to keep the cooking manuals, worksheets, and Meal Inventory Checklist (*Worksheet G*).**

    A manual for each cook really is a must. Putting your manual up high will keep it cleaner and easier to find.

2. **Start assembling entrees.**

    Our method is simple:

    She does the beef.
    I do the chicken.
    We share the rest.

    We each choose a recipe card and then check the Tally Sheet (*Worksheet D*) to see how many of this entree we are making. Then we follow that column on the recipe card and begin assembling. We ask the other cook how they want each recipe packaged (pans, bags, rigid containers). Then we assemble the recipe, package it and get it into the freezer. This way, you can finish 1 recipe and get it into the freezer at once. Besides the sense of accomplishment, the quality of the food is better because you have gotten it into the freezer as quickly as possible. The chances of cross-contamination from meats is also greatly reduced this way.

STEP 6
ASSEMBLE ENTREES & STOCK FREEZER

❖ Assembly Day Tips:

1. Get plenty of sleep the night before (at least 4 hours☺).
2. Freeze soupy casseroles first so they can freeze on a level surface in the freezer.
3. Start time-consuming, slow cooking, or marinated foods early.
4. Do the most complicated recipes early while you have the most energy and concentration power.
5. Assemble in large quantities. For example, don't make each individual quiche one at a time. Combine the ingredients for 6 quiches and then pour out the filling evenly. This method will save you many hours.
6. Think about which days are your busiest and pre-bake a few items for those days.
7. When possible, line baking sheets and pans with foil for easier cleanup of pre-baked recipes.
8. Use as few pots, bowls, and utensils as possible and wash or rinse them off between recipes. Wash well between raw meats and egg recipes.
9. Cover your work surfaces with several layers of newspaper to make end-of-the-day cleanup easier.
10. Make sure you freeze only enough to be consumed at one time or you will be getting tired of leftovers.
11. Label all foods clearly. Many of the foods will look the same once they are in the freezer.
12. When cooking with a partner, be sure to include your name when labeling your entrees. Believe us, you won't want to sort this all out again later. It also helps to put your food on different shelves or, if possible, in different freezers.
13. COOL FOODS AS QUICKLY AS POSSIBLE AND FREEZE AS QUICKLY AS POSSIBLE.
14. Foods can be cooled by placing the hot dish in a tub or sink full of cold water, in a cooler of ice, or even in the refrigerator, if you must. We have even placed covered pans into snow banks!
15. Storing all of your frozen food on this day may be tricky for some, especially in the summer. Freezer chests with ice packs may help. Neighbors are usually willing to loan you a shelf or or two of freezer space for awhile, also.
16. For us, the visiting cook usually leaves her food at the host cook's house another day or two until it is frozen solid. Then it is much easier to transport.
17. Just a warning - the morning seems to go by before you feel like you have anything done. At about halfway through the afternoon it all starts coming together.
18. Wear good, supportive shoes and plan to change them halfway through the day with another pair.
19. Tall stools are helpful to keep you off your feet while working.
20. Keep conversations positive and uplifting!
21. Play upbeat music to help you keep your pace.
22. Take a lunch break. We often buy muffins and fruit to snack on throughout the day.
23. Be clean. Shower, wash your hair, and pull it back. No one enjoys hair in their food, especially if it came from your friend's head. Wash your hands frequently, especially after coming into contact with raw meats. Using a different pair of disposable latex gloves for each recipe is even better.
24. Don't answer the phone on Assembly Day. Chances are it's going to be:
    a) a window salesman, b) a gabby friend you haven't talked to for 6 months,
    c) someone asking you to do something, or d) a wrong number.
25. If the kids are there, keep them happy. Check out a new pile of books. Rent a special video. Set up a snack and beverage table just for them that they can visit all day.

STEP 6
ASSEMBLE ENTREES & STOCK FREEZER

3. Fill out Freezer Inventory Checklist *(Worksheet G)* as you put your labeled entrees into the freezer. If you make more than 12 recipes, use two inventory checklists.

Worksheet G Sample
MEAL INVENTORY CHECKLIST
Date __4/8__

As you prepare your entrees for the freezer, fill in one of these checklists for each cook (sometimes you end up with more than you planned). Each cook should take her checklist home and put it on her refrigerator (or some equally conspicuous place).

Directions: Place a slash mark in one box for each entree as it goes into the freezer. ☑

(This way you can always know how many total entrees you have.)

Then cross it off, ☒, as you remove the entree to serve it.

	RECIPE	NEED ON HAND
☒☒☑☐☐☐	1. Taco Rice	shredded cheese, tortillas
	serve with green salad, carrot sticks, peach slices	
☒☒☑☐☐☐	2. Crock Pot Beef	sandwich buns
	serve with broccoli or green beans, fruit salad	
☒☒☑☐☐☐	3. Parsley Parmesan Chick.	
	serve with make ahead mashed potatoes, slaw, apple sauce	
☒☒☑☑☐☐	4. Chicken in marinade	coals for grill
	serve with baked potato or corn on the cob, fruit slush, carrots	
☒☒☑☐☐☐	5. Sausage Rice bake	parmesan cheese
	serve with spinach salad, stir fry veggies, champagne salad	
__16__	TOTAL MEALS	

STEP 7
CLEAN UP & EVALUATE

One of us usually begins the cleanup while the other is finishing the last recipe. It will take longer than you think. At this point, your feet will probably be aching and you'll be a bit slap happy, but knowing that you have 24-30 main dish entrees ready will feel GREAT!

We try to do a quick evaluation of what went right and wrong. How did it go? What will you do differently next time? Writing down these observations will really help you for your next Assembly Day. Be sure to write recipe changes on your cards for next time. Save your worksheets from each of your cooking adventures, also. You'll be surprised how handy this information will be later on.

That's it! You're done! Congratulations and welcome to 30 DAY GOURMET COOKING!!

30 DAY GOURMET
MEAL PLANNING CALENDAR

We have included this calendar to aid you in daily meal planning. Fill in the dates on this calendar and make notes of what you want to serve on the especially busy days. Also make note of when you will have company and what you plan to serve. Mark vacations and any frozen entrees you would like to take along. Filling these events in BEFORE you even choose your recipes would be especially helpful. If you fill in what side dishes you plan to serve with each entree, grocery shopping will be even easier and more efficient. We grant you permission to photocopy the calendar for your own use. Happy Cooking!

Sunday	Monday	Tuesday	Wednesday	Thursday	Friday	Saturday
	1 ballet 4:30 Chicken Fingers make ahead potatoes jello, carrot sticks	2 soccer 4:00 Taco Rice salad, peaches	3 Choir 7p Beef sandwiches buns, oven fries green beans	4 soccer 4:00 Turkey/Noodles carrot salad fruit slush	5 piano recital 7-9 Swiss Steak mashed potatoes	6 game 8 am Lazy Day Lasagna salad, broccoli
7 Chicken Normandy mashed potatoes mixed vegetables	8 ballet 4:30 Burgers, home fries, coleslaw apple raisin salad	9 soccer 4:00 Pizza w/team	10 Choir 7p Ham Loaf sauce #1 gramette's dressing Champagne salad	11 soccer 4:00 Tetrazzini broccoli salad fruit cocktail	12 Chicken in marinade - grill out - corn, baked potatoes	13 game 2:00 p Meat loaf potato hash fruit slush
14 Mom & Dad eating here - Double amounts of Savory Baked Chicken	15 ballet 4:30 Pork Barbecue sandwiches buns, corn, broccoli	16 soccer 4:00 Spaghetti garlic bread green salad	17 Choir 7p Shepherds pie sautéed apples	18 soccer 4:00 Turkey/Noodles carrot salad apple sauce	19 D's B/day Dinner Eat at Mom's	20 game 8 am Sausage Rice Bake - peaches spinach salad
21 Swiss Steak baked potatoes broccoli casserole	22 ballet 4:30 West Country Cod wild rice dressing	23 soccer 4:00 Ham Loaf Crispy Cheese pot. asparagus	24 Choir 7p Hungarian Goulash acid potatoes Hard rolls cooked carrots	25 soccer 4:00 Turkey & gravy Gramettes dressing	26 Mediterranian chicken price mixed vegetables	27 game 10 am Pizza w/team
28 Chicken Normandy mashed potatoes mixed vegetables	29 ballet 4:30 Dinner at Mom's - Bring frozen salad	30 soccer 4:00 Marinated Chicken - broiled cheese stix	31 Choir 7p Cheese filled shells french bread green salad			

24

30 DAY GOURMET
PLANNING WORKSHEETS

❖ You will use these each time you cook so keep this set as master copies.

❖ We suggest that you copy 5-10 of each at a time (less of C, more of D). You know how quickly a month can fly by.

❖ Please ONLY make copies for yourself. When your friends start begging for your organizational secrets, give them our toll free number or address.   Thanks!

WORKSHEET A
PLANNING DAY WORKSHEET

Planning Day _____   Planning Time _____

Where? _____

Kids' Activities? _____

What to bring: ☐ 5-10 recipes my family likes
                        ☐ *Worksheet B* (inventory list of my ingredients on hand)
                        ☐ Calendar to decide shopping and assembly days
                        ☐ Other: _____
                        _____
                        _____
                        _____

Shopping Day _____   Assembly Day _____

Permission to photocopy for manual owner.

WORKSHEET B
ON HAND INVENTORY SHEET

ITEMS IN STOCK

Item Name	Quantity?	Where?	Cost?
1.			
2.			
3.			
4.			
5.			
6.			
7.			
8.			
9.			
10.			
11.			
12.			
13.			
14.			
15.			
16.			
17.			
18.			
19.			
20.			
21.			
22.			
23.			
24.			
25.			

WORKSHEET C
RECIPE

Recipe: _____

Meals:	1	2	3	4	5	6

serves _____

Ingredients:

_____	_____	_____	_____	_____	_____	___
_____	_____	_____	_____	_____	_____	___
_____	_____	_____	_____	_____	_____	___
_____	_____	_____	_____	_____	_____	___
_____	_____	_____	_____	_____	_____	___
_____	_____	_____	_____	_____	_____	___
_____	_____	_____	_____	_____	_____	___
_____	_____	_____	_____	_____	_____	___
_____	_____	_____	_____	_____	_____	___
_____	_____	_____	_____	_____	_____	___
_____	_____	_____	_____	_____	_____	___

Containers: _____

Assembly Directions:

_____
_____
_____
_____
_____

Freezing and Cooking Directions:

_____
_____
_____
_____
_____
_____

Comments:

_____
_____
_____

	Seafood					Dairy						Canned Food Items												
Fillets	esh Fillets		Eggs	Margarine	Butter	Sour Cream																		

uce		Fresh Produce						Staples - Spices										
					Flour	Oil	Ketchup	Non-Stick Spray	Gallon Freezer Bags									

30 DAY GOURMET

Worksheet D
TALLY SHEET

Directions:
1. Write the name of your first recipe on line 1 and line 1a. Fill in how many meals of each recipe you will need for each cook.
2. In the diagonal columns, fill in the needed ingredients.
    Going horizontally across lines 1 and 1a, fill in the appropriate amounts of each ingredient.
3. Next, write down the name of your next recipe on lines 2 and 2a. Again, going across the Tally Sheet, write in the appropriate ingredients and the amounts of each. Do the same for all your recipes. Be sure to account for any freezer bags, spray oils, etc. . .needed for your recipes on your assembly day.
4. After ALL of your ingredients have been accounted for, going down the chart vertically, tally the TOTAL AMOUNT NEEDED of each ingredient. For example; total all the ground beef and put that number in the "*total needed*" box under ground beef. Total all the boneless chicken breasts needed and place that number in the "*total needed*" box under boneless chicken breast.
5. Get out the On Hand Inventory Sheet (*Worksheet B*) that each cook brings to the planning session. Cross off the items you already have and write them onto your list of What To Bring On Assembly Day (*Worksheet G*). This eliminates the guesswork of who promised to bring the oatmeal or salt.
6. Refer back to the Tally Sheet *(Worksheet D)*. In the "*total on hand*" box, subtract the ingredients that each of you will be bringing to cooking day (refer to *Worksheet B*) and write in your totals.
7. Continue on with the steps on page 13 of the planner.

| Recipe Title | Meals For Cook #1 | Meals For Cook #2 | Food Type | | Beef | | | Chicken | | | Turkey | | | Por |
			Ground Beef, Fresh	Ground Beef Frozen	Boneless Breast	Chicken Parts	Cooked Diced	Whole Turkey	Ground Turkey	Turkey Breast	Cooked Diced	Ground Pork	Ham	Pork Sausage	Bacon	Frozen
1.																
2.																
3.																
4.																
5.																
6.																
7.																
8.																
9.																
10.																
11.																
12.																
Total Needed																
(-) Total on Hand																
(=) Total to Buy																

Recipe Title	Meals For Cook #1	Meals For Cook #2	Food Type	Grains, Pasta, Dry Beans, Breads, Crumb Crackers	Frozen Proc
1.a					
2.a					
3.a					
4.a					
5.a					
6.a					
7.a					
8.a					
9.a					
10.a					
11.a					
12.a					
Total Needed					
(-) Total on Hand					
(=) Total to Buy					

WORKSHEET E
SHOPPING LIST

Beef
_____
_____
_____
_____
_____

Chicken
_____
_____
_____
_____
_____

Turkey
_____
_____
_____
_____

Pork
_____
_____
_____

Fish
_____

Dairy
_____
_____
_____
_____
_____
_____
_____

Canned Foods
_____
_____
_____
_____
_____
_____
_____
_____
_____
_____

Grains
_____
_____
_____

Pasta
_____
_____

Breads
_____
_____
_____

Dry Beans
_____
_____
_____
_____

Frozen Produce
_____
_____
_____
_____
_____
_____

Fresh Produce
_____
_____
_____
_____
_____

Staples
_____
_____
_____
_____
_____
_____
_____
_____

Spices
_____
_____
_____
_____
_____
_____
_____
_____

Miscellaneous
_____
_____
_____
_____
_____
_____
_____
_____
_____
_____

WORKSHEET F
WHAT TO DO & BRING

WHAT TO DO BEFORE ASSEMBLY DAY

*Fill out this sheet during your planning session. You will need one for each cook.

Cook #1 _____   Cook #2 _____

1. _____   1. _____
2. _____   2. _____
3. _____   3. _____
4. _____   4. _____
5. _____   5. _____
6. _____   6. _____
7. _____   7. _____
8. _____   8. _____
9. _____   9. _____
10._____   10._____

WHAT TO BRING ON ASSEMBLY DAY

*Before your planning session ends, decide who will bring what items to the kitchen where Assembly Day will take place. Remember, just one missing item could cost you a few hours☺.

*Include your "On Hand Inventory" items needed as well as appliances, pots, bowls, and containers for your meals.

Cook #1 _____   Cook #2 _____

1. _____   1. _____
2. _____   2. _____
3. _____   3. _____
4. _____   4. _____
5. _____   5. _____
6. _____   6. _____
7. _____   7. _____
8. _____   8. _____
9. _____   9. _____
10._____   10._____

WORKSHEET G
MEAL INVENTORY CHECKLIST

Date _____

	RECIPE	NEED ON HAND
☐☐☐☐☐☐	1. _____	_____
	serve with _____	
☐☐☐☐☐☐	2. _____	_____
	serve with _____	
☐☐☐☐☐☐	3. _____	_____
	serve with _____	
☐☐☐☐☐☐	4. _____	_____
	serve with _____	
☐☐☐☐☐☐	5. _____	_____
	serve with _____	
☐☐☐☐☐☐	6. _____	_____
	serve with _____	
☐☐☐☐☐☐	7. _____	_____
	serve with _____	
☐☐☐☐☐☐	8. _____	_____
	serve with _____	
☐☐☐☐☐☐	9. _____	_____
	serve with _____	
☐☐☐☐☐☐	10. _____	_____
	serve with _____	
☐☐☐☐☐☐	11. _____	_____
	serve with _____	
☐☐☐☐☐☐	12. _____	_____
	serve with _____	
_____	TOTAL MEALS	

Menu Planner

Month/Year _____

Sunday	Monday	Tuesday	Wednesday	Thursday	Friday	Saturday

30 DAY GOURMET

30 DAY GOURMET
BEEF ENTREES

❖ Taco Rice
❖ Crock Pot Beef Sandwiches
❖ Spaghetti Sauce
❖ Lazy Day Lasagna
❖ Crock Pot Hungarian Goulash
❖ Master Meat Mix:
   Meatloaf
   Meatballs

❖ Swiss Steak
❖ Shepherd's Pie
❖ Sloppy Joe Casserole
❖ Marinade for Beef
❖ 7 Sauces
❖ Beef Cube Mix:
   Western Beef Stew
   Beef Stroganoff

TIPS FOR BEEF ENTREES

T. = Tablespoon t. = teaspoon C. = Cup lb. = pound oz. = ounce	As always, if you have any questions, please call, write, or e-mail us. We will try to get an answer to you as soon as possible. Phone: 1-800-9-MANUAL e-mail: office@30daygourmet.com

☑ One pound of fresh ground beef will yield approximately 2 1/2-3 Cups of browned beef.

☑ 1/4 pound of fresh beef is considered to be a standard serving. Adjust the portions you freeze to fit your family's needs.

☑ We use a cookie scoop with a spring mechanism to form meatballs. Much quicker!

☑ Remember, if you buy ahead and freeze beef, you should cook it thoroughly before re-freezing. For example, frozen ground beef is thawed, browned, then used in a recipe like *Sloppy Joe Casserole*, then frozen. If you want to use the frozen ground beef for a meatloaf, meatballs, or patties, it must be thoroughly cooked (no pink in the center) before re-freezing.

←Healthy Tips→

We hope that you will find the recipes in this pack to be nutritious, tasty, simple and completely freezable. We are not dietitians, but by way of our own fat-reducing, nutrition-lifting journey, have gained some knowledge and practical application in serving great tasting and good-for-you foods.
In all of the following recipes, feel free to substitute lower fat or fat free products wherever you choose. Some that we make regularly are:

INSTEAD OF:	TRY:
mayonnaise or salad dressing	lowfat/fat free mayo & salad dressing
whole or 2% milk	skim milk
regular sour cream	fat free sour cream
eggs	liquid/frozen egg substitutes
high fat cheese	low fat or less cheese
high fat dressings	fat free dry & pourable dressings
ground beef	turkey or *TVP (texturized vegetable protein)
white pastas & flour	whole wheat pasta & flour (1/2 -all)

*TVP: If you are trying to cut your fat and cholestrerol, try using TVP as a partial or complete ground beef substitute. This product can be purchased through health food stores and food co-ops. It comes in small rice-sized pieces that can be soaked in vegetable or fat free broths and used in place of ground beef. This is a very high protein, low fat and economical substitute. 2 1/2 cups of dry TVP are equal to 2 1/2 cups of cooked ground meat or 1 pound of fresh beef. If you fear the reaction of the people you feed, try mixing 1/4 TVP to 3/4 cooked ground meat - this is usually a good way to begin.

Recipe: Taco Rice

Meals:	1	2	3	4	5	6
serves 4-6						

Ingredients:

	1	2	3	4	5	6
ground beef, chicken or turkey (uncooked)	1 lb.	2 lbs.	3 lbs.	4 lbs.	5 lbs.	6 lbs.
onion, diced	1 C.	2 C.	3 C.	4 C.	5 C.	6 C.
taco seasoning packet	1	2	3	4	5	6
canned tomatoes	16 oz.	32 oz.	48 oz.	64 oz.	80 oz.	96 oz.
white or brown rice, cooked	2 C.	4 C.	6 C.	8 C.	10 C.	12 C.
cheese, shredded	2 C.	4 C.	6 C.	8 C.	10 C.	12 C.

Containers: Freezer bags or containers suitable for your family. We often do some small (for snacks) and some large (for meals).

Assembly Directions:
Brown meat and drain. Combine meat, onion, taco seasoning packet(s), cooked rice and tomatoes in saucepan. Simmer until thick - about 30 minutes.

Freezing and Cooking Directions:
Cool, label, and freeze in bags or rigid containers. Also freeze a ziptop bag with 2 C. of shredded cheese for each meal. **To serve,** thaw completely. For taco salad, warm over medium heat. Serve with lettuce, taco chips, tomatoes, sour cream and the enclosed cheese.

Comments:
This stuff is great! We use it for main entrees and snacks to fill taco shells or to fill flour tortillas for burritos. Melted cheese on top of corn chips and Taco Rice makes yummy nachos.

Recipe: Crock Pot Beef (for sandwiches)

Meals: serves 6-8	1	2	3	4	5	6

Ingredients:

beef roast, chuck roast or thick chuck steak, fat trimmed	2 1/2 lbs.	5 lbs.	7 1/2 lbs.	10 lbs.	12 1/2 lbs.	15 lbs.
dry Italian or Ranch salad dressing packets or onion soup mix packets	2	4	6	8	10	12
water	1 C.	2 C.	3 C.	4 C.	5 C.	6 C.

On Hand:

buns or hoagie rolls	8	16	24	32	40	48

Containers: quart size ziptop freezer bags or 2 1/2 C. rigid freezer containers

Assembly Directions:

In a cold crock pot, place the thawed or fresh roast. Pour the contents of the salad dressing or soup packets over the meat. Pour the water over all. Cover crock pot with lid. Can be cooked overnight on low heat or 6 hours on high heat until meat shreds easily with a fork. When done, turn off crock pot and uncover it to cool quickly.

Freezing and Cooking Directions:

When cooled, place meat and juice in a freezer bag or container. Seal, label and freeze. (2 cups fills 8 average sized buns.)

To serve, thaw and heat in a microwave or saucepan over medium heat until warmed through. Serve over rolls or in buns.

Comments:

Roasts over 7 1/2 lbs. may not fit well in a crock pot. Try to borrow an extra crock pot if you choose to make more than 7 1/2 lbs.

This is a large recipe and we divide each recipe in half for freezing purposes. About 1/4-1/3 C of cooked meat is a serving.

Barbecue Option: *Reduce water by half. Pour water and 1 C. of barbecue sauce per recipe over all. (May add more barbecue sauce later to taste.)*

Recipe: Spaghetti Sauce

Meals:	1	2	3	4	5	6
serves 4-6						

Ingredients:

	1	2	3	4	5	6
ground beef, uncooked	1 lb.	2 lbs.	3 lbs.	4 lbs.	5 lbs.	6 lbs.
onion, diced	1/2 C.	1 C.	1 1/2 C.	2 C.	2 1/2 C.	3 C.
garlic, minced	2t.	1 T.+1 t.	2 T.	2 T.+2 t.	3 T.+1 t.	4 T.
green pepper, minced (optional)	1/2 C.	1 C.	1 1/2 C.	2 C.	2 1/2 C.	3 C.
tomato sauce	8 oz.	16 oz.	24 oz.	32 oz.	40 oz.	48 oz.
tomato paste	6 oz.	12 oz.	18 oz.	24 oz.	30 oz.	36 oz.
water	1 C.	2 C.	3 C.	4 C.	5 C.	6 C.
oregano	1 t.	2 t.	1 T.	1 T. + 1 t.	1 T. + 2 t.	2 T.
basil	1/4 t.	1/2 t.	3/4 t.	1 t.	1 1/4 t.	1 1/2 t.
sugar (optional)	1 t.	2 t.	1 T.	1 T. + 1 t.	1 T. + 2 t.	2 T.
pepper	1/4 t.	1/2 t.	3/4 t.	1 t.	1 1/4 t.	1 1/2 t.

Containers: Gallon ziptop freezer bags or 6 cup freezer containers

Assembly Directions:

Brown beef and drain. Combine with remaining ingredients in a saucepan or crock pot. Simmer one hour in saucepan or 6 hours to overnight in crock pot. Cool completely. The longer this sauce simmers the thicker it gets.

Freezing and Cooking Directions:

Pour cooled sauce into freezer bags or freezer containers. Label and freeze. Before serving, thaw completely. Heat in a saucepan over medium heat or in microwave.

Comments:

We use this for spaghetti, lasagna, goulash, manicotti, cheese-filled shells and *pizza casserole among other things. The hardest part of all these meals is having the sauce made.
*Pizza Casserole: Nanci's kids love this! Just spread 32 oz (4 cups) of sauce in the bottom of a 9x13 pan. Sprinkle 2 C. of shredded cheddar or mozzarella cheese over sauce. Place 2 cans of refrigerator biscuits (20) on top. Bake at 350° for 30 minutes.

Recipe: Lazy Day Lasagna

Meals:	1	2	3	4	5	6
serves 6						
Ingredients:						
cottage cheese	12 oz.	24 oz.	36 oz.	48 oz.	60 oz.	72 oz.
mozzarella cheese, shredded	2 C. (8 oz.)	4 C. (16 oz.)	6 C. (24 oz.)	8 C. (32 oz.)	10 C. (40 oz.)	12 C. (48 oz.)
eggs	2	4	6	8	10	12
parsley, chopped	1/3 C.	2/3 C.	1 C.	1 1/3 C.	1 2/3 C.	2 C.
onion powder	1 t.	2 t.	1 T.	1 T.+1 t.	1 T.+2 t.	2 T.
dried basil leaves	1/2 t.	1 t.	1 1/2 t.	2 t.	2 1/2 t.	1 T.
pepper	1/8 t.	1/4 t.	1/4 t.+1/8 t.	1/2 t.	1/2 t.+1/8 t.	3/4 t.
*spaghetti sauce (homemade or purchased)	32 oz.	64 oz.	96 oz.	128 oz.	160 oz.	192 oz.
ground beef or ground turkey, cooked	3/4 C.	1 1/2 C.	2 1/4 C.	3 C.	3 3/4 C.	4 1/2 C.
lasagna noodles, regular, uncooked	9	18	27	36	45	54
water	3/4 C.	1 1/2 C.	2 1/4 C.	3 C.	3 3/4 C.	4 1/2 C.

On Hand: grated parmesan cheese
Containers: 12x8x2" baking dish

Assembly Directions:

In large bowl, mix cheeses, eggs, parsley, onion powder, basil, and pepper until well blended; set aside.
In medium bowl, mix together spaghetti sauce and cooked ground beef.
In 12x8x2" baking dish, spread 3/4 C. meat sauce. Layer 3 uncooked noodles and top with meat sauce. Spread with 1/2 of cottage cheese mixture and 1 1/2C. meat sauce. Layer 3 more noodles on top of meat sauce. Spread with remaining cottage cheese mixture. Top with remaining 3 uncooked noodles and remaining meat sauce. Pour water around edges.

Freezing and Cooking Directions:

Wrap tightly with freezer paper, foil, or place dish in 2 gallon ziptop bag. Label and freeze.
To serve, thaw and bake covered at 375° for 45 minutes. Uncover and bake an additional 15 minutes. Let stand 10 minutes. Serve with parmesan cheese. To bake from the frozen stage, add 30 minutes to total baking time.
*See our Spaghetti Sauce recipe in *Beef Entrees*.

Recipe: Crock Pot Hungarian Goulash

Meals:	1	2	3	4	5	6
serves 6-8						
Ingredients:						
lean stew beef	2 lb.	4 lbs.	6 lbs.	8 lbs.	10 lbs.	12 lbs.
olive oil	2 T.	1/4 C.	1/4 C.+2T.	1/2 C.	1/2 C.+2T.	3/4 C.
salt and pepper to taste						
paprika	1 t.	2 t.	1 T.	1 T.+1 t.	1 T.+2 t.	2 T.
garlic, minced	1 t.	2 t.	1 T.	1 T.+1 t.	1 T.+2 t.	2 T.
tomato paste	6 oz.	12 oz.	18 oz.	24 oz.	30 oz.	36 oz.
allspice	1/8 t.	1/4 t.	3/8 t.	1/2 t.	1/2t.+1/8t.	3/4 t.
water	1/2 C.	1 C.	1 1/2 C.	2 C.	2 1/2 C.	3 C.

On Hand: potatoes

Containers: gallon freezer bags or containers suitable for your family

Assembly Directions:
Cut beef in 2" cubes. (We buy stew meat but cut it even smaller for the kids. Easier now than later!) Brown in olive oil. Season with salt, pepper, and paprika. Stir well and add garlic, tomato paste, allspice and water. Simmer covered 2 hours or in crock pot 6-8 hours.

Freezing and Cooking Directions:
Cool, label, and freeze in bags or rigid containers.
To serve, thaw and place goulash mixture in a large saucepan. Cube one potato per person and add to goulash mixture. Simmer over medium/low heat. Cook until potatoes are tender, about 15 minutes.
Option: . Meat and sauce may be served over mashed, or baked potatoes.

Optional Crock Pot Directions: Place goulash and potatoes in a crock pot and simmer 3-4 hours.

Comments:
This is very different from the Italian-type goulash. It can cook by itself on assembly day! Great as leftovers!

Recipe: Master Meat Mix

Meals: serves 4-6	5 C.mix= 1 pan or 60 mtballs	10 C.= 2 pans or 120 mtballs	15 C.= 3 pans or 180 mtballs	20 C.= 4 pans or 240 mtballs	25 C.= 5 pans or 300 mtballs	30C.= 6 pans or 360 mtbs.
Ingredients:						
beef, pork, turkey- ground (any 1 or a mixture)	1 1/2 lbs.	3 lbs.	4 1/2 lbs.	6 lbs.	7 1/2 lbs.	9 lbs.
dry oats or cooked brown rice	2/3 C.	1 1/3 C.	2 C.	2 2/3 C.	3 1/3 C.	4 C.
onion, diced	1/2 C.	1 C.	1 1/2 C.	2 C.	2 1/2 C.	3 C.
salt	1 t.	2 t.	1 T.	1 T.+1 t.	1 T.+2 t.	2 T.
garlic powder	1/2 t.	1 t.	1 1/2 t.	2 t.	2 1/2 t.	1 T.
eggs	2	4	6	8	10	12
ketchup or tomato sauce	2/3 C.	1 1/3 C.	2 C.	2 2/3 C.	3 1/3 C.	4 C.

Containers: gallon ziptop bags, 6 cup freezer containers or loaf pans

Assembly Directions:

Mix all ingredients very well with your hands (you may want to wear rubber or disposable gloves) in a large bowl. We have used big, plastic storage containers to do this when making a large quantity. We use this mixture primarily for meatloaf and meatballs. See the Meatloaf & Meatballs recipes in *Beef Entrees*.

MEATLOAF

See our Master Meat Mix recipe in *Beef Entrees*. 5 cups of this mix will fill a standard meatloaf pan.

Assembly Directions:
Form 5 C. of Master Meat Mix into a loaf in a loaf pan, packing well. Bake at 350° for 1 hour or until no pink shows in the center of the loaf. Cool and chill. Slice meatloaf, if desired.

Freezing and Cooking Directions:
Wrap, label and freeze. On serving day, thaw completely. If it has not been done previously, slice the meatloaf then lay the slices flat on a baking sheet coated with non-stick cooking spray. Brush with one of the optional sauces, if desired. Bake at 350° for 15 minutes or until thoroughly heated.

OR

For every 4 adult servings, place 5 C. of Master Meat Mix in a ziptop freezer bag or rigid freezer container. On serving day, thaw completely and press well into loaf shape in a standard loaf pan. Bake as above. (Don't freeze raw meat unless it was fresh, not frozen, when you began.)
Cool loaf for 10 minutes before slicing.

MEATBALLS

Assembly Directions:
Using 5 C. of the Master Meat Mix, form approximately 60 meatballs about the size of large walnuts (or use a small cookie scoop). Place the meatballs on an oiled, (you can use foil if you want to save on clean-up) rimmed baking sheet. Broil until lightly browned and no longer pink in the center. Cool.

Freezing and Cooking Directions:
Place meatballs in a freezer bag or container. Seal, label and freeze.
To serve, thaw meatballs and bake at 350° for 10-20 minutes until hot.
If using one of the optional sauces, thaw meatballs and pour sauce over the meatballs. Bake for 20-30 minutes. Turn the meatballs in the sauce occasionally during the cooking time. These can be served as is or over rice, pasta or potatoes.

Comments:
For some odd reason, meatballs seem to go over better with our kids than a slice of meatloaf even though the meat is exactly the same. Go figure!

OPTIONAL SAUCES FOR MEATBALLS & MEATLOAF

Each of these sauces is formulated to be used with one meal (5 C.) of our Master Meat Mix. These sauces can be poured over broiled meatballs then baked for 20-30 minutes at 350°. The sauces can be poured over a meatloaf before the last 30 minutes of baking time. Gently turn meatballs in the sauce once or twice during baking to coat them and baste the meatloaf every ten minutes during the last half hour.

If you choose to pre-bake and slice a meatloaf before freezing, we recommend making the sauce on the day it is to be served. The sauce can be brushed over the meatloaf slices during warming and the excess sauce warmed and passed around at the table. For all of these sauces, mix all of the ingredients together, unless otherwise noted.

SALISBURY SAUCE: 1 1/2   C. *white sauce (or one 10 3/4 oz.can cream of mushroom soup diluted with 1/4 C. water), plus 2 t. Worcestershire sauce.

BARBECUE SAUCE   1 1/2 C. of any commercial or homemade barbecue sauce.

ITALIAN SAUCE   2-3 C. of meatless spaghetti sauce can be poured over the baking meatballs and served on spaghetti noodles. 1 1/2 C. sauce can be used on a meatloaf.

STROGANOFF SAUCE   Pour 1 1/2 C. of *white sauce or one 10 3/4 oz. can cream of mushroom soup over meatballs. Just before serving, gently stir in 8 oz. sour cream.

TERIYAKI SAUCE

1/2 C. soy sauce	1/2 C. brown sugar
2 t. vinegar	2 t. cooking oil
1/2 t. ground ginger	1 minced garlic clove

SAVORY SAUCE   Two 10 3/4 oz. cans tomato soup
2 t. Worcestershire sauce
1 1/4 C. water

Halve this recipe for meatloaf.

SWEDISH SAUCE

5 T. Worcestershire sauce	4 T. any vinegar
2 T. sugar	1 C. ketchup
1/3 C. water	

COMMENTS:
Any of these sauces will help make the average meatloaf taste just WONDERFUL!
Using different ones could let you serve the same meat once a week but make it taste different each time. Give some a try!
*See white sauce recipe in Side Dishes/Misc. Section.

Recipe: Swiss Steak

Meals: serves 3-4	1	2	3	4	5	6
Ingredients:						
cubed steaks	1 1/2 lbs.	3 lbs.	4 1/2 lbs.	6 lbs.	7 1/2 lbs.	9 lbs.
flour	1/3 C.	2/3 C.	1 C.	1 1/3 C.	1 2/3 C.	2 C.
salt	1/2 t.	1 t.	1 1/2 t.	2 t.	2 1/2 t.	1 T.
celery, diced	2/3 C.	1 1/3 C.	2 C.	2 2/3 C.	3 1/3C.	4 C.
onion, diced	1/2 C.	1 C.	1 1/2 C.	2 C.	2 1/2 C.	3 C.
green or red pepper, diced	1 C.	2 C.	3 C.	4 C.	5 C.	6 C.
tomato soup	10 oz.	20 oz.	30 oz.	40 oz.	50 oz.	60 oz.
water	3/4 C.	1 1/2 C.	2 1/4 C.	3 C.	3 3/4 C.	4 1/2 C.
Worcestershire sauce	1 T.	2 T.	3 T.	1/4 C.	1/4 C.+1 T.	1/4 C.+2T.

Containers: ziptop freezer bags
Assembly Directions:
Mix the flour and salt. Coat the meat on both sides with the flour and place in a ziptop bag or freezer container and seal. Saute or steam the vegetables until tender. Mix the veggies with the soup, water and Worcestershire sauce Place the sauce in a quart size ziptop bag or container and seal.

Freezing and Cooking Directions:
Label and freeze both containers.
To serve, thaw both bags or containers thoroughly. In a sprayed casserole, place 1/2 C. sauce then alternate layers of meat and sauce, pouring all extra sauce over top of the meat. Cover the pan and bake at 350° for 45-60 minutes or microwave on high for 10 minutes then on medium for 35-40 minutes until the meat is tender and no longer pink in the center. If you choose to microwave, be sure to have it revolve while cooking or turn the pan several times during cooking.
Crock Pot cooking: Layer meat and sauce as above and let it cook 6-8 hours until done.

Comments:
Tara usually microwaves this dish and serves it with rice. The meat was very tender. Nanci baked hers the first time and served it with mashed potatoes. She thought it could be more tender and now does it in the crock pot or microwave.
If your kids hate the veggies, either puree them in the blender or food processor or leave them in large, one-inch chunks that can be easily removed.

Recipe: Shepherd's Pie

Meals: serves 4-6	1	2	3	4	5	6
Ingredients:						
butter/margarine	2 T.	1/4 C.	6 T.	1/2 C.	1/2 C.+2T.	3/4 C.
onion, chopped	1/2 C.	1 C.	1 1/2 C.	2 C.	2 1/2 C.	3 C.
carrots, chopped	2	4	6	8	10	12
flour	1 T.	2 T.	3 T.	1/4 C.	1/4 C.+1T.	1/4 C.+2T.
beef broth	2 C. (16 oz.)	4 C. (32 oz.)	6 C. (48 oz.)	8 C. (64 oz.)	10 C. (80 oz.)	12 C. (96 oz.)
tomato sauce	1/2 C.	1 C.	1 1/2 C.	2 C.	2 1/2 C.	3 C.
Worcestershire sauce	1 t.	2 t.	1 T.	1 T.+ 1 t.	1 T. + 2 t.	2 T.
oregano	1/4 t.	1/2 t.	3/4 t.	1 t.	1 1/4 t.	1 1/2 t.
salt and pepper to taste						
ground beef or turkey, cooked	2 1/2 C.	5 C.	7 1/2 C.	10 C.	12 1/2 C.	15 C.
*make ahead mashed potatoes	2 C.	4 C.	6 C.	8 C.	10 C.	12 C.

Containers: 8" pie plate(s), 8"x8" pan(s) or gallon ziptop for filling and quart ziptop for potatoes

Assembly Directions:
Melt butter/margarine in saucepan and fry the onion and carrots until golden brown. Stir in the flour and cook one minute. Gradually stir in beef broth and bring to a boil, stirring constantly. Add the tomato sauce, Worcestershire sauce, oregano and seasonings. Cover the pan. Reduce heat and simmer 15 minutes. Remove from heat and add cooked ground meat. Mix well. Pour into sprayed 8x8 pan, 8" pie plate or ziptop bag. If in pan or plate, top with potatoes, wrap with freezer paper, foil, or place in a 2 gallon ziptop bag. Seal. If in bag, put potatoes in separate bag, label and freeze together.

Freezing and Cooking Directions:
Label and freeze.

To serve, thaw. (If in bags, put filling in pan and spread potatoes on top.)

Bake at 400° for 20-30 minutes or until topping is brown and meat is heated through.

To heat from the frozen stage, add 10-15 minutes more baking time.

Comments:
If you like your pie drier, reduce the amount of beef broth.

*See Make Ahead Mashed Potato Recipe in *Side Dishes/Misc. Section.*

Recipe: Sloppy Joe Casserole

Meals:	1	2	3	4	5	6
serves 4-6						

Ingredients:

	1	2	3	4	5	6
salad shell macaroni	8 oz	16 oz.	24 oz.	32 oz.	40 oz.	48 oz.
sloppy joe mix envelope	1 small	2 small	3 small	4 small	5 small	6 small
ground beef or ground turkey, cooked	1 1/4 C.	2 1/2 C.	3 3/4 C.	5 C.	6 1/4 C.	7 1/2 C.
tomato sauce	8 oz.	16 oz.	24 oz.	32 oz.	40 oz.	48 oz.
tomato paste	6 oz.	12 oz.	18 oz.	24 oz.	30 oz.	36 oz.
water	1 C.	2 C.	3 C.	4 C.	5 C.	6 C.
cottage cheese	16 oz.	32 oz.	48 oz.	64 oz.	80 oz.	96 oz.
cheddar cheese, shredded	1 C. 4 oz.	2 C. (8 oz.bag)	3 C. (12 oz.bag)	4 C. (16 oz. bag)	5 C. 20 oz.	6 C. (24 oz.bag)

Containers: 2 1/2 qt. casserole dish or 8x8 baking dish. Because of the layers we usually don't "bag" this recipe but you could if you bagged the pasta and the meat sauce and kept the cottage and cheddar cheese on hand.

Assembly Directions:
Cook macaroni half the recommended time. Drain. Combine seasoning mix with the ground beef or turkey, tomato sauce, tomato paste, and 1 cup water. In sprayed 2 1/2 qt. casserole dish, layer half the macaroni, half the cottage cheese and half the meat sauce; repeat. Top with shredded cheddar cheese. Wrap dish in freezer paper, foil, or place dish in 2 gallon ziptop bag.

Freezing and Cooking Directions:
Label and freeze.
To serve, thaw and bake uncovered at 350° for 40-50 minutes or until bubbling or place frozen casserole in oven and bake 1 hour 20 minutes.

Comments:
When made with ground turkey or VERY lean ground beef and non-fat cheeses, this recipe only has 1 gram of fat per serving.

Recipe: Marinade for Beef (for steaks, stir fry strips, kabob chunks, etc.)

Meals: serves 4-6	**1**	**2**	**3**	**4**	**5**	**6**
Ingredients:						
beef	2-3 lbs.	4-6 lbs.	6-9 lbs.	8-12 lbs.	10-15 lbs.	12-18lbs.
Marinade: lemon juice	1/3 C.	2/3 C.	1 C.	1 1/3 C.	1 2/3 C.	2 C.
Worcestershire sauce	1/4 C.	1/2 C.	3/4 C.	1 C.	1 1/4 C.	1 1/2 C.
dry mustard	2 T.	1/4 C.	1/4 C.+2T.	1/2 C.	1/2 C.+2T	3/4 C.
Accent (opt.)	1/2 t.	1 t.	1 1/2 t.	2 t.	2 1/2 t.	1 T.
oil (any kind)	1 C.	2 C.	3 C.	4 C.	5 C.	6 C.
*red wine vinegar	1/2 C.	1 C.	1 1/2 C.	2 C.	2 1/2 C.	3 C.
*soy sauce (lite &/or reduced salt works fine)	1/2 C.	1 C.	1 1/2 C.	2 C.	2 1/2 C.	3 C.
black pepper	1 T.	2 T.	3 T.	1/4 C.	1/4 C.+1 T.	1/4 C.+2T
garlic, minced	2 t.	1 T.+1 t.	2 T.	2 T.+2 t.	3 T.+1 t.	4 T.

Containers: gallon freezer bags or rigid containers suitable for your family.

Assembly Directions:
Cut beef into suitable strips or pieces. Place in freezer bags or rigid containers.
Combine all marinade ingredients. Pour into ziptop freezer bags or containers over meat. (Each meal makes approximately 3 cups.)

Freezing and Cooking Directions:
Label and freeze. Thaw at room temperature or in microwave. Grill or cook beef. Discard marinade.

Comments:
If you like variety, do this recipe! Marinated meat is so great to have around. You can decide later what to do with it - the hard part is getting it into the marinade! And if you think meat that has marinated 4 hours tastes good, wait until you try meat that has marinated for 3 weeks!
*We usually buy these items in bulk from a restaurant supply store. It is incredibly cheaper and easier to use than the little bottles.

Recipe: Master Beef Cube Mix and Sauce

Meals:	4 meals or 16 C. (serves 4-5)	8 meals or 32 C. (serves 8-10)	12 meals or 48 C. (serves 12-15)
Ingredients:			
lean stew beef	5 lbs.	10 lbs.	15 lbs.
onion soup mix	1 packet	2 packets	3 packets
bay leaves	2	4	6
*fat free, beef flavored white sauce	6 C.	12 C.	18 C.
mushrooms, minced	1/4 C.	1/2 C.	3/4 C.
celery, minced	1/4 C.	1/2 C.	3/4 C.
water	2 C.	4 C.	6 C.

Containers: gallon freezer bags or rigid containers

Assembly Directions:
Combine all of the above ingredients in a large Dutch oven or covered roasting pan. Stir well. Bake at 300° for about 4 hours or until meat is tender.

Freezing and Cooking Directions:
Cool the mix and pour it into freezer ziptops or rigid containers. Leave about 1/2" space at top of rigid containers. Label and freeze.
To serve, thaw and serve heated over pasta, rice or potatoes or with *Western Beef Stew or *Beef Stroganoff.

Comments:
*See fat free white sauce recipe in *Side Dishes/Misc. Section.*
*See Western Beef Stew recipe in *Beef Entrees.*
*See Beef Stroganoff recipe in *Beef Entrees.*

Recipe: Western Beef Stew

Meals:	1	2	3	4	5	6
serves 4-6						

Ingredients:

	1	2	3	4	5	6
*beef cube mix	4 C.	8 C.	12 C.	16 C.	20 C.	24 C.
potatoes, diced	5 med.	10 med.	15 med.	20 med.	25 med.	30 med.
carrots, diced	2 1/2 C.	5 C.	7 1/2 C.	10 C.	12 1/2 C.	15 C.
onion, thinly sliced	1 small	2 small	3 small	4 small	5 small	6 small
celery, chopped	1/2 C.	1 C.	1 1/2 C.	2 C.	2 1/2 C.	3 C.
mushrooms	4 oz.	8 oz.	12 oz.	16 oz.	20 oz.	24 oz.
beef or vegetable broth	1/2 C.	1 C.	1 1/2 C.	2 C.	2 1/2 C.	3 C.

Containers: gallon freezer bags or rigid containers suitable for your family

Assembly Directions:
Combine potatoes and carrots in a large saucepan. Add just enough water to cover vegetables. Cook 12-15 minute:
until tender. In a small saucepan, saute onion and celery in broth until slightly tender. Add mushrooms and saute two
more minutes. (In microwave, steam onion and celery in covered container with small amount of water or broth
until soft. Add mushrooms and steam an additional two minutes.) Drain liquid from potatoes and carrots.
Add vegetables to potatoes and carrots. Stir in beef cube mix.

Freezing and Cooking Directions:
Cool stew and pour it into freezer ziptops or rigid containers. Leave about 1/2" space at top of rigid containers
Label and freeze.
To serve, thaw beef stew. Simmer about 15-20 minutes until heated through.

Variation: Beef Stew Pie
Put ingredients in a 9x13 baking pan or two pie dishes. Top with a pie crust. Flute edges. Cut slits in crust. Wrap in
freezer paper, foil, or place dish in 2 gallon freezer bag. Freeze.
To serve, thaw and bake at 400° for 30-45 minutes. (May be baked first, then frozen, thawed and reheated.)

Comments:
*See Master Beef Cube Mix in *Beef Entrees*.

Recipe: Beef Stroganoff

Meals:	1	2	3	4	5	6
Serves 4-6						

Ingredients:

	1	2	3	4	5	6
*beef cube mix	4 C.	8 C.	12 C.	16 C.	20 C.	24 C.

On Hand:

	1	2	3	4	5	6
sour cream	2 C.	4 C.	6 C.	8 C.	10 C.	12 C.

noodles, potatoes, or rice

Containers: Gallon freezer bags or rigid containers suitable for your family.

Assembly and Cooking Directions:

This entree assembles quickly on the day you will serve it. Thaw the frozen beef cube mix. Warm the beef in a saucepan. Just before serving, stir in the sour cream. Serve over hot noodles, cooked rice or potatoes.

Comments:

This tastes much better when combined "fresh" rather than stirring it all up together on cooking day and freezing it

*See Master Beef Cube Mix in *Beef Entrees.*

30 DAY GOURMET
CHICKEN/TURKEY ENTREES

- ❖ Parsley Parmesan Chicken
- ❖ Chicken Enchilada Casserole
- ❖ Crispy Rice Chicken
- ❖ Chicken/Turkey Divan
- ❖ Mediterranean Chicken & Rice
- ❖ Marinades for Chicken

- ❖ Savory Baked Chicken
- ❖ Tetrazzini
- ❖ Turkey & Noodles
- ❖ Chicken Normandy
- ❖ Chicken/Turkey Patties
- ❖ Chicken Fingers

TIPS FOR POULTRY ENTREES

T.	= Tablespoon
t.	= teaspoon
C.	= Cup
lb.	= pound
oz.	= ounce

As always, if you have any questions, please call, write, or e-mail us. We will try to get an answer to you as soon as possible.
Phone: 1-800-9-MANUAL
e-mail: office@30daygourmet.com

☑ We often substitute diced turkey breast for diced chicken. The turkey is so much easier to buy, boil and bone than all those various parts. We think it is the cheapest, too.

☑ Don't buy leaking packages. The meat should not be swimming in juices.

☑ Don't let raw meat juices run onto any other foods. Always clean surfaces, mixing bowls, utensils, and hands well after working with raw poultry.

☑ Fresh poultry should not have any noticeable odor.

☑ When boiling poultry to dice or slice, pour VERY HOT WATER over the meat. Hot water will seal in the juices and flavor.

☑ When boiling poultry to make a flavorful broth, pour COLD water over the meat. This helps extract the meat flavor.

☑ A large enameled or aluminum water bath canner is very useful. It will hold 2-3 turkey breasts or whole chickens. Placing a trivet or wire rack in the bottom will keep the meat from sticking.

☑ Heavy duty latex gloves or "chicken gloves" as we like to call them, are great for boning and handling hot meat. The meat will come off much quicker when it's hot.

☑ We buy packages of specific parts rather than mixed fryer parts for recipes like "Parsley Parmesan Chicken". It's hard to find a 3-legged bird if your 3 kids all want a leg.

☑ One breast, or two smaller pieces constitutes an adult serving in our recipes.

☛Healthy Tips☚

* We always plan for extra diced, cooked poultry to use in nutritious salads and sandwiches. We freeze it in 2-cup portions.
* Use fat-free broth whenever possible. Wouldn't you rather consume your fat in hot fudge sundaes than in chicken broth??
* Try our fat free white sauce recipe to replace creamed soups in your own recipes. Betcha won't know the difference!
* We bake or broil our chicken instead of frying it. Of course, we also remove skin or start with skinless meat. You can really reduce the fat just by following these two rules of thumb.

Recipe: Parsley Parmesan Chicken

Meals: serves 4-6	1	2	3	4	5	6
Ingredients:						
Italian salad dressing	1/4 C.	1/2 C.	3/4 C.	1 C.	1 1/4 C.	1 1/2 C.
fresh fryer parts	2-3 lbs.	5-6 lbs.	8-9 lbs.	11-12 lbs.	14-15 lbs.	17-18 lbs.
grated parmesan cheese	1/2 C.	1 C.	1 1/2 C.	2 C.	2 1/2 C.	3 C.
dry bread crumbs	1/3 C.	2/3 C.	1 C.	1 1/3 C.	1 2/3 C.	2 C.
parsley flakes	2 T.	1/4 C.	1/3 C.	1/2 C.	2/3 C.	3/4 C.
paprika	1/2 t.	1 t.	1 1/2 t.	2 t.	2 1/2 t.	1 T.
salt	1/2 t.	1 t.	1 1/2 t.	2 t.	2 1/2 t.	1 T.
pepper	1/4 t.	1/2 t.	3/4 t.	1 t.	1 1/4 t.	1 1/2 t.

Containers: gallon freezer bags for chicken, quart freezer bags for crumbs

Assembly Directions:

To Pre-Bake on Cooking Day: Pour salad dressing in a large bowl. Add the chicken parts to the dressing, coating well. Cover and chill about 4 hours, or overnight. Turn chicken in the dressing occasionally.

Combine parmesan cheese, dry bread crumbs, parsley flakes, paprika, salt and pepper in a shallow bowl. Roll chicken one piece at a time in the crumbs, then place chicken in a greased 9x 13 baking pan or on a cookie sheet. Spoon excess dressing over the chicken. Bake at 350° for 1 hour, or until thickest piece is done.

To Bake on Serving Day: Pour chicken parts and salad dressing into a ziptop freezer bag. Combine the parmesan cheese, dry bread crumbs, parsley flakes, paprika, salt and pepper and pour into a quart-sized freezer bag. Attach to the bag of chicken or put both bags into a larger freezer bag.

Freezing and Cooking Directions:

Pre-Baked Chicken:

Remove from oven and cool. Put baked chicken pieces into a freezer bag or rigid container. Label and freeze.
To serve, place chicken in a 9x13 baking dish or pan. Warm in 400° oven for 10 minutes or until warmed through.
Non-Baked Chicken:

Seal, label, and freeze. **To serve,** thaw marinated chicken and crumb mixture. Roll chicken one piece at a time in the crumbs, or shake in a bag, then place chicken in a greased 9x13 pan or on a cookie sheet. Spoon excess dressing over the chicken. Bake at 350° for 1 hour or until thickest piece is done.

Comments:

Having the chicken already baked can really come in handy if you don't have an hour before dinnertime. Diet dressing works fine. Foil-lined cookie sheets help speed the clean up if you bake lots of chicken on assembly day.

Recipe: Chicken Enchilada Casserole

Meals:	1	2	3	4	5	6

serves 6-8 (1 recipe makes 2-9" rounds or 1 9x13 pan)

Ingredients:

	1	2	3	4	5	6
10" four tortillas	4	8	12	16	20	24
chicken; cooked, diced	3 C.	6 C.	9 C.	12 C.	15 C.	18 C.
*white sauce, chicken flavored	6 C.	12 C.	18 C.	24 C.	30 C.	36 C.
cheddar cheese, shredded	1 C.	2 C.	3 C.	4 C.	5 C.	6 C.

Containers: 2-9" round pans/dishes, 9x13 pan, or freezer ziptop bags

Assembly Directions:
Place 1 Cup of white sauce in the bottom of 9" round dishes or 9x13 pan and spread to moisten the bottom layer Tear or cut tortillas into strips for 9x13 or square pans. For round pans, tortillas may be left whole. Place 1/2 the tortilla strips or 1 whole tortilla into the bottom of the pan. Layer 1/2 the chicken on the tortillas. Pour 1/2 the sauce over the chicken. Repeat the layers, ending with sauce. Sprinkle cheese over top.

Freezing and Cooking Directions:
Wrap tightly with freezer paper, foil, or place in 2 gallon ziptop bag. (An 8" or 9" pie pan will fit in a gallon ziptop freezer bag.)
To serve, thaw and bake at 350° for 20-30 minutes. If this recipe is frozen in a metal or rigid plastic container, it can be popped out frozen and placed in a glass or microwave safe pan and thawed in the microwave 20 minutes, then baked in the oven. If you do this, you may want to put the cheese in a separate ziptop bag (for obvious reasons!).
To bake from the frozen stage, add 10-15 minutes extra baking time.

Comments:
We don't recommend pre-cooking this on assembly day since it bakes so quickly.
*Options: *Enchiladas: 1/3 of the white sauce may be stirred into the chicken and used as a filling to roll enchiladas. Spread 1/4-1/3 C. chicken/sauce mixture in each tortilla and roll up. Place each roll seam side down in a spray-treated or greased pan. Top with remaining sauce, then sprinkle on the cheese. Bake as directed above.*
+OR, freeze the chicken and sauce together. Thaw, warm and serve over potatoes, rice, biscuits, or pasta. Yummy!

*See white sauce and fat free white sauce recipes in our *Side Dishes/Misc. Section.*

Recipe: Crispy Rice Chicken

Meals:	1	2	3	4	5	6
serves 4-6						
Ingredients:						
fresh fryer parts	2-3 lbs.	5-6 lbs.	8-9 lbs.	11-12 lbs.	14-15 lbs.	17-18 lbs.
eggs, beaten	1	2	3	4	5	6
water	1/2 C.	1 C.	1 1/2 C.	2 C.	2 1/2 C.	3 C.
crispy rice cereal, coarsely crushed	1 1/2 C.	3 C.	4 1/2 C.	6 C.	7 1/2 C.	9 C.
garlic powder	1/2 t.	1 t.	1 1/2 t.	2 t.	2 1/2 t.	1 T.
salt	1/2 t.	1 t.	1 1/2 t.	2 t.	2 1/2 t.	1 T.
pepper	1/4 t.	1/2 t.	3/4 t.	1 t.	1 1/4 t.	1 1/2 t.

Containers: gallon freezer ziptop bags or rigid containers

Assembly Directions:
To Pre-Bake on Cooking Day
Rinse and pat dry fryer parts. Beat the egg and water together in a shallow bowl. Place cereal crumbs in another shallow bowl and mix in the garlic powder, salt, and pepper. Dip the fryer parts in the egg mixture, then roll in the crumb mixture to coat all sides. Place each piece in a spray treated or foil-lined 9x13 baking pan, or shallow baking dish. Pre-bake 45 minutes at 350° or until juices run clear. Cool.
To Bake on Serving Day
Prepare chicken and coat as above. Do not bake.

Freezing and Cooking Directions:
Pre-Baked Chicken:
Remove from oven and cool. Put baked chicken pieces into a freezer bag or rigid container. Label and freeze.
To serve, place chicken in a 9x13 baking dish or pan. Finish baking at 350° for 20-30 minutes until hot and browned.
Non-Baked Chicken:
Place coated chicken in gallon freezer ziptop bags or rigid containers. Label and freeze. If using ziptop bags, you may want to "open freeze" the chicken first. Place chicken on a baking sheet and put in freezer until firm. Remove and put into freezer bags. This will help keep the coating on the chicken and will keep the pieces from freezing to each other.
To serve, thaw coated chicken pieces and place in spray treated or foil-lined 9x13 pan or shallow baking dish. Bake uncovered at 350° for 1 hour.

Comments:
Having the chicken already baked can really come in handy if you don't have an hour before dinnertime. Foil-lined cookie sheets help speed the clean up if you bake lots of chicken on assembly day.

Recipe: Chicken/Turkey Divan

Meals:	1	2	3	4	5	6

serves 6 (1 recipe makes 2-9" rounds or 1-9x13 pan)

Ingredients:

Ingredient	1	2	3	4	5	6
cooked rice, white or brown	3 C.	6 C.	9 C.	12 C.	15 C.	18 C.
fresh chicken breast fillets	8	16	24	32	40	48
OR						
cooked, diced chicken or turkey	6 C.	12 C.	18 C.	24 C.	30 C.	36 C.
mayonnaise,	1 C.	2 C.	3 C.	4 C.	5 C.	6 C.
*white sauce,chicken flavored	3 C.	6 C.	9 C.	12 C.	15 C.	18 C.
OR						
cream soup, canned (chicken, mushroom, or broccoli)	21 oz.	42 oz.	63 oz.	84 oz.	105 oz.	126 oz.
lemon juice	2 T.	1/4 C.	1/3 C.	1/2 C.	2/3 C.	3/4 C.
broccoli, frozen (chopped or spears)	20 oz.	40 oz.	60 oz.	80 oz.	100 oz.	120 oz.
cheddar cheese, grated	1 C.	2 C.	3 C.	4 C.	5 C.	6 C.

Containers: 2-9" round pans/dishes or 9x13 pan or freezer ziptops

Assembly Directions:
Cook and dice chicken or turkey if using diced poultry. Cook rice 1/2 the recommended time. Cook broccoli. Set aside. Mix lemon juice and mayonnaise, then add chicken flavored white sauce. Spread rice in container. Layer on broccoli, then half the sauce, then the chicken, then remaining sauce. Top with grated cheese.

Freezing and Cooking Directions:
Wrap tightly with freezer paper, foil, or 2 gallon ziptop bag. Seal,label and freeze.
To serve, thaw and bake at 350° for 30 minutes or until chicken is tender and easily pierced with a fork.

Comments:
We don't recommend pre-cooking this on assembly day since it bakes so quickly.
If using chopped poultry, you can mix all the ingredients together except the cheese. Freeze rice, chicken, broccoli and sauce in one bag and cheese topping in another. When ready to serve, thaw then pour into casserole. Top with cheese and bake.
*See white sauce and fat free white sauce recipes in our Side Dishes/Misc. Section.

Recipe: Mediterranean Chicken & Rice

Meals:	1	2	3	4	5	6
serves 4-6						

Ingredients:

	1	2	3	4	5	6
boneless chicken breasts or fryer parts (fresh or frozen)	7	14	21	28	35	42
olive oil	1/4 C.	1/2 C.	3/4 C.	1 C.	1 1/4 C.	1 1/2 C.
garlic, minced	1 t.	2 t.	1 T.	1 T. + 1 t.	1 T. + 2 t.	2 T.
onion, chopped	1/2 C.	1 C.	1 1/2 C.	2 C.	2 1/2 C.	3 C.
gr. pepper, chopped (optional)	1 1/2 C.	3 C.	4 1/2 C.	6 C.	7 1/2 C.	9 C.
red pepper (optional)	1/4 t.	1/2 t.	3/4 t.	1 t.	1 1/4 t.	1 1/2 t.
tomatoes, crushed	8 oz.	16 oz.	24 oz.	32 oz.	40 oz.	48 oz.
chicken broth	3 1/2 C.	7 C.	10 1/2 C.	14 C.	17 1/2 C.	21 C.

On Hand:

	1	2	3	4	5	6
quick rice, uncooked	1 1/2 C.	3 C.	4 1/2 C.	6 C.	7 1/2 C.	9 C.

Packaging: gallon freezer ziptops or rigid containers.

Assembly Directions:
Brown chicken breast in olive oil. Add garlic, onions, and pepper (optional). Add tomatoes. Simmer till fork tender or till juices run clear. Cool. Place chicken mixture in freezer bags or containers. Pour broth over top.
Seal, label and freeze.

Optional: Measure out rice and put in ziptop bag. Attach to chicken and sauce.

Freezing and Cooking Directions:
Freeze chicken and sauce in rigid containers or ziptop bags. Label.
To serve, thaw chicken and sauce. Place uncooked rice in bottom of baking pan. Arrange chicken pieces over rice Pour sauce over all. Bake uncovered at 350° for 45-50 minutes. Do not stir casserole.

Recipe: Debbie's (Tara's Sister in law) Chicken Marinade

Meals:	1	2	3	4	5	6
serves 4-6						

Ingredients:

	1	2	3	4	5	6
boneless, skinless chicken breasts .	7 pcs.	14 pcs.	21 pcs.	28 pcs.	35 pcs.	42 pcs.

Marinade:

	1	2	3	4	5	6
salt	2 t.	1 T.+1 t.	2 T.	2 T.+2 t.	3 T.+1 t.	4 T.
*Worchestershire sauce	1/4 C.	1/2 C.	3/4 C.	1 C.	1 1/4 C.	1 1/2 C.
dry mustard	2 T.	1/4 C.	1/4 C.+2T.	1/2 C.	1/2 C.+2 T.	3/4 C.
oil (any kind)	1 C.	2 C.	3 C.	4 C.	5 C.	6 C.
*red wine vinegar	1/2 C.	1 C.	1 1/2 C.	2 C.	2 1/2 C.	3 C.
*soy sauce (lite &/or reduced salt works fine)	3/4 C.	1 1/2 C.	2 1/4 C.	3 C.	3 3/4 C.	4 1/2 C.
pepper	1 t.	2 t.	1 T.	1 T.+1 t.	1 T.+2 t.	2 T.
garlic, minced	1 t.	2 t.	1 T.	1 T.+1 t.	1 T.+2 t.	2 T.
parsley flakes	1 1/2 t.	1 T.	1 T.+1 1/2 t.	2 T.	2 T.+1 1/2 t.	3 T.

Containers: gallon freezer bags or rigid containers suitable for your family

Assembly Directions:
Combine all marinade ingredients. Place chicken pieces in ziptop or container. Pour marinade over the meat. (Each meal makes approximately 3 cups.)

Freezing and Cooking Directions:
Label and freeze.
To serve, thaw. Grill or cook chicken. Discard marinade.
For Chicken Strips: Cut chicken breasts into strips and marinade to use for stir fry , fajitas, or hot off the grill!

Comments:
Great to have on hand for grilling season or anytime! (Nanci makes her husband clean snow off the grill to serve this in the winter!) Also a wonderful company meal. Just pull out two or three bags instead of one!
*We usually buy these items in bulk from a restaurant supply store. It is incredibly cheaper and easier to use than the little bottles.

Recipe: Teriyaki Chicken Marinade for Stir Fry

Meals:	**1**	**2**	**3**	**4**	**5**	**6**
serves 4						
Ingredients:						
boneless, skinless chicken breasts (sliced into 1/4" thin strips)	1 1/2 lbs.	3 lbs.	4 1/2 lbs.	6 lbs.	7 1/2 lbs.	9 lbs.
Marinade:						
ginger, powdered	1/4 t.	1/2 t.	3/4 t.	1 t.	1 1/4 t.	1 1/2 t.
dry mustard	2 t.	1 T.+1 t.	2T.	2 T.+2 t.	3 T.+1 t.	1/4 C.
oil (any kind)	1/4 C.	1/2 C.	3/4 C.	1 C.	1 1/4 C.	1 1/2 C.
*soy sauce (lite &/or reduced salt works fine)	1/2 C.	1 C.	1 1/2 C.	2 C.	2 1/2 C.	3 C.
garlic, minced	1 t.	2 t.	1 T.	1 T.+1 t.	1 T.+2 t.	2 T.
molasses	2 T.	1/4 C.	1/4 C.+2 T.	1/2 C.	1/2 C.+2 T.	3/4 C.

On Hand: 1-1 1/2 C. thin sliced, raw vegetables per adult (zucchini, onions, carrots, spinach, bok choy, mushrooms celery, peppers, bamboo shoots, etc., in any combination) and rice or pasta
Containers: gallon freezer bags or rigid containers suitable for your family

Assembly Directions:
Combine all marinade ingredients. Place chicken strips in ziptop or container. Pour marinade over the meat. (Each meal makes approximately 1 C.)

Freezing and Cooking Directions:
Label and freeze.
To serve, thaw the meat and marinade. Heat 2 T. olive oil in a large skillet over medium high heat. A drop of water should sizzle rapidly when dropped into the hot pan. Drain the marinade from the meat and discard. Add the meat strips and cook them rapidly, stirring frequently. Chicken should no longer be pink in the center, but don't overcook. Overcooking will make the meat tough. When cooked, remove the meat from the skillet with a spatula or spoon and keep warm in a covered dish.
Add the vegetables to the hot skillet in order of density. The denser vegetables need to cook the longest. Carrots and onions first, then peppers, celery and bok choy about three minutes later, and last add the more tender selections like spinach and zucchini. Stirring constantly, cook the vegetables to the desired amount of doneness. The meat may be stirred back into the pan, or served separately. Serve with hot cooked rice or pasta.

Comments:
Rice or pasta may be cooked ahead of time and frozen in ziptop bags for an even faster meal. Just reheat in the microwave!

Recipe: Savory Baked Chicken

Meals:	1	2	3	4	5	6
serves 4-6						
Ingredients:						
boneless chicken breasts, chopped (fresh) in 1" strips	7	14	21	28	35	42
*white sauce, chicken flavored	3 C.	6 C.	9 C.	12 C.	15 C.	18 C.
OR						
canned cream of chicken soup	21 oz.	42 oz.	63 oz.	84 oz.	105 oz.	126 oz.
grated parmesan cheese	1/4 C.	1/2 C.	3/4 C.	1 C.	1 1/4 C.	1 1/2 C.
parsley flakes	1 t.	2 t.	1 T.	1 T.+1 t.	1 T.+2 t.	2 T.
oregano	1/4 t.	1/2 t.	3/4 t.	1 t.	1 1/4 t.	1 1/2 t.
basil	1/4 t.	1/2 t.	3/4 t.	1 t.	1 1/4 t.	1 1/2 t.
pepper	1/8 t.	1/4 t.	3/8 t.	1/2 t.	1/2 t.+1/8 t.	3/4 t.
spaghetti, uncooked	8 oz.	16 oz.	24 oz.	32 oz.	40 oz.	48 oz.
On Hand: chicken broth	14 oz.	28 oz.	42 oz.	56 oz.	70 oz.	84 oz.

Containers: gallon and quart freezer ziptop bags, 8x8 dish or 2 1/2 qt. casserole to serve

Assembly Directions:
Chop fresh boneless chicken pieces and put into freezer bag. Label.
Combine white sauce or soup, parmesan cheese, parsley flakes, oregano, basil and pepper. Bag and label.
Spray skillet with cooking spray and heat to medium-high. When pan is hot, pour in pasta, broken in 1" pieces
Watch pasta, turning frequently until golden brown. Remove from heat. When cooled, bag and label. Put all 3 bags
together inside a large freezer ziptop bag and label it *Savory Baked Chicken*.

Freezing and Cooking Directions:
Freeze.
To serve, thaw 3 bags. An hour before serving, preheat oven to 350°. Spray an 8x8 baking dish or a 2 1/2 qt
casserole. Place chicken in dish and pour thawed sauce on top. Bake 1 hour or until pieces are tender. 35-40
minutes into baking time, pour broth (on hand) into skillet. Bring to boil, then add broken pasta. Reduce to simmer
and cook until tender. To serve, place chicken pieces on top of pasta on plate. Pass the sauce at the table.

Comments:
*This sounds complicated, but it's SO good! Just be sure to plan this for a night when you have an hour before
dinner.*
*See white sauce recipes in *Side Dishes/Misc. Section*.

Recipe: Chicken or Turkey Tetrazzini

Meals: serves 4-6	1	2	3	4	5	6

Ingredients:

	1	2	3	4	5	6
*white sauce, chicken flavored **OR**	6 C.	12 C.	18 C.	24 C.	30 C.	36 C.
canned cream of mushroom soup	42 oz.	84 oz.	126 oz.	168 oz.	210 oz.	252 oz.
lemon juice	2 T.	1/4 C.	1/3 C.	1/2 C.	2/3 C.	3/4 C.
green pepper, diced (opt.)	1/2 C.	1 C.	1 1/2 C.	2 C.	2 1/2 C.	3 C.
spaghetti, broken in 1" pieces & cooked	8 C.	16 C.	24 C.	32 C.	40 C.	48 C.
cooked chicken or turkey, diced	4 C.	8 C.	12 C.	16 C.	20 C.	24 C.
mushrooms (opt.)	8 oz.	16 oz.	24 oz.	32 oz.	40 oz.	48 oz.
grated parmesan cheese	1 C.	2 C.	3 C.	4 C.	5 C.	6 C.

Containers: 2 1/2 qt. casserole or gallon and quart freezer ziptop bags

Assembly Directions:

Combine white sauce or soup and lemon juice. Saute (in a small amount of oil) or steam green pepper and add to sauce. Break spaghetti into 1" pieces and boil in salted water 1/2 the recommended time. Drain spaghetti. Mix spaghetti, chicken or turkey, and mushrooms into sauce.
Optional: Cook spaghetti full recommended time and put in ziptop bag. Attach to chicken and sauce. Stir into casserole just before baking.

Freezing and Cooking Directions:

Pour mixture into 2 1/2 qt. casserole and top with grated parmesan cheese. Wrap in freezer paper, foil, or place pan in 2 gallon ziptop bag. Label and freeze. OR Pour mixture into gallon ziptop freezer bag. Enclose a small freezer bag with 1 C. grated parmesan cheese for each recipe. Label and freeze.
To serve, thaw completely. If in microwave-safe container, heat on medium power 20-30 minutes, or until hot throughout. If in metal pan, bake at 350° 45-60 minutes or until thoroughly heated. If food is in a freezer bag thaw, pour contents into baking dish, sprinkle enclosed cheese on top, and cook as above.
Frozen casserole may be baked for 1 1/2 hours at 350°.

Recipe: Turkey and Noodles

Meals:	1	2	3	4	5	6

serves 6-8

Ingredients:

Ingredient	1	2	3	4	5	6
*turkey or chicken broth	96 oz.	192 oz.	288 oz.	384 oz.	480 oz.	576 oz.
salt	1/2 t.	1 t.	1 1/2 t.	2 t.	2 1/2 t.	1 T.
onion, diced	1/2 C.	1 C.	1 1/2 C.	2 C.	2 1/2 C.	3 C.
pepper	1/4 t.	1/2 t.	3/4 t.	1 t.	1 1/4 t.	1 1/2 t.
frozen egg noodles (or homemade style)	1 lb.	2 lb.	3 lb.	4 lb.	5 lb.	6 lb.
flour	1/4 C.	1/2 C.	3/4 C.	1 C.	1 1/4 C.	1 1/2 C.
milk	1 1/2 C.	3 C.	4 1/2 C.	6 C.	7 1/2 C.	9 C.
cooked, diced turkey	4 C.	8 C.	12 C.	16 C.	20 C.	24 C.

salt to taste

Containers: gallon freezer ziptops or rigid containers

Assembly Directions:
In large pot, heat broth to boiling. Add salt, onion, and pepper. Add frozen noodles and bring again to a boil. Reduce heat to keep from boiling over, but still bubbling freely. Cook 10 minutes. Stir flour and milk together and add to bubbling pot. Cook until juices are somewhat reduced and slightly thickened. Add meat. Salt to taste. Cool.

Freezing and Cooking Directions:
Divide into family sized portions in freezer containers or ziptop bags. Leave 1/2" space at top of container. Seal and freeze.
To serve, thaw and reheat over low heat in saucepan, in microwave, or in 350° oven 20-30 minutes.

Comments:
Canned or frozen peas, or cooked, sliced carrots may be added with the meat. Add 1-1 1/2 C. per recipe.
**For low fat turkey broth, save broth from cooked turkey. Chill it. Remove fat that has risen to the top. Doing this will also save you lots of money!*

30 DAY GOURMET
CHICKEN ENTREE

Recipe: Chicken Normandy

Meals:	1	2	3	4	5	6
serves 4-6						
Ingredients:						
chicken breasts or fryer parts	7	14	21	28	35	42
olive or vegetable oil	2 T.	1/4 C.	3/8 C.	1/2 C.	1/2 C.+2 T.	3/4 C.
onion, diced	1/2 C.	1 C.	1 1/2 C.	2 C.	2 1/2 C.	3 C.
flour	1/4 C.	1/2 C.	3/4 C.	1 C.	1 1/4 C.	1 1/2 C.
apple cider or white cooking wine	12 oz.	24 oz.	36 oz.	48 oz.	60 oz.	72 oz.
chicken broth	4 oz.	8 oz.	12 oz.	16 oz.	20 oz.	24 oz.
oregano	1/2 t.	1 t.	1 1/2 t.	2 t.	2 1/2 t.	1 T.
rosemary	1/4 t.	1/2 t.	3/4 t.	1 t.	1 1/4 t.	1 1/2 t.
salt & pepper to taste						
cooking apples	4	8	12	16	20	24

Containers: 3 quart casserole, 9x13 baking dish or pan, or gallon freezer ziptop bags

Assembly Directions:

To Pre-Bake: Over medium-high heat, heat oil in a frying pan. Add the chicken and fry on both sides until golden brown. Remove and place in 3 qt. casserole or 9x13 pan. Lower heat to medium-low. Add onion to the pan and fry until tender. Sprinkle in flour and cook, stirring constantly, until light brown. Gradually stir in apple cider or cooking wine, broth, herbs and bring to a boil. stirring constantly. Cook until thickened. Season to taste with salt and pepper and pour over chicken. Peel and core apples and cut into thick slices. Place apple slices on top of chicken and sauce Cover casserole. Bake at 350° for 1 hour or until just tender. Cool, wrap in foil, freezer paper, or place pan in 2 gallon ziptop freezer bag. Label and freeze.

To Bake on serving day: Cook chicken and sauce as above. Place browned chicken in gallon ziptop bag or rigid container. Pour cooled sauce and sliced apples into another freezer ziptop bag. Put both bags inside a larger ziptop Label and freeze.

Freezing and Cooking Directions:

Pre-baked chicken: To serve, reheat the frozen casserole (without thawing) covered at 400° for 1 hour or until heated through.

Ziptop bagged chicken: To serve, thaw bags. Place chicken pieces in 3 qt. casserole or 9x13 dish/pan. Pour sauce over chicken. Arrange apple slices on top. Bake covered at 350° for 1 hour.

Comments:

This is really yummy! The apples give it a great taste!

30 DAY GOURMET
CHICKEN ENTREE

Recipe: Chicken/Turkey Patties

Meals:	12 patties	24 patties	36 patties	48 patties	60 patties	72 patties
Ingredients:						
*cooked chicken or turkey, finely minced	4 C.	8 C.	12 C.	16 C.	20 C.	24 C.
eggs, lightly beaten	4	8	12	16	20	24
grated parmesan cheese	1 C.	2 C.	3 C.	4 C.	5 C.	6 C.
fine, dry bread crumbs	1/2 C.	1 C.	1 1/2 C.	2 C.	2 1/2 C.	3 C.
olive or canola oil	2 T.	1/4 C.	6 T.	1/2 C.	1/2 C.+2 T.	3/4 C.

On Hand: For parmigiana; spaghetti sauce and shredded mozzarella cheese

Containers: freezer ziptop bags or rigid containers

Assembly Directions:
Combine all the ingredients well. Use your hands to make 12 oval patties, 1/2-1" thick. Heat the oil in a skillet Saute the patties on each side until browned. (This may also be done under the broiler.) Cool thoroughly.

Freezing and Cooking Directions:
Freeze in ziptop bags or rigid containers.
To serve, thaw and reheat in a skillet, microwave, or oven at 350° for about 10 minutes.
For Parmigiana: On the day you will eat it, thaw the patties. In a flat bottomed baking dish, place 1/2 C. spaghett sauce. Spread this evenly over the bottom of the dish. Place the patties in the pan, one at a time, topping each patty with 2T. or so of spaghetti sauce, and 2 T. or so mozzarella cheese. The patties should overlap each other slightly Pour as much additional sauce as you wish over the patties evenly. Top with additional shredded mozzarella cheese if you like. Heat in a 350° oven for 30-40 minutes, or until heated through.

Comments:
This recipe has become a tradition in both of our families. It is delicious, versatile and VERY easy. These are good as sandwiches, or served with gravy and potatoes or ketchup and fries, and even as Parmigiana.

*The cooked chicken is easily minced in a food processor. A blender and food grinder would do fine, but to do it by hand would be very tedious.

Recipe: Baked Chicken Fingers/Nuggets

Meals: serves 4-6	**36** **fingers**	**72** **fingers**	**108** **fingers**	**144** **fingers**	**180** **fingers**	**216** **fingers**
Ingredients:						
boneless, skinless chicken breasts (cut into lengthwise strips or chunks)	2 lbs.	4 lbs.	6 lbs.	8 lbs.	10 lbs.	12 lbs.
Sauce #1:						
mayonnaise	1/4 C.	1/2 C.	3/4 C.	1 C.	1 1/4 C.	1 1/2 C.
dry mustard	2 t.	1 T.+1 t.	2 T.	2 T.+2 t.	3 T.+1 t.	1/4 C.
onion powder	1 t.	2 t.	1 T.	1 T.+1 t.	1 T.+2 t.	2 T.
OR						
Sauce #2:						
milk	1/2 C.	1 C.	1 1/2 C.	2 C.	2 1/2 C.	3 C.
ranch dressing;bottled	1/2 C.	1 C.	1 1/2 C.	2 C.	2 1/2 C.	3 C.
Coating:						
bread crumbs or cracker meal	1 C.	2 C.	3 C.	4 C.	5 C.	6 C.
paprika	1/2 t.	1 t.	1 1/2 t.	2 t.	2 1/2 t.	1 T.

Containers: gallon freezer bags or rigid containers suitable for your family.

Assembly Directions:

Choose one sauce, then mix all of its ingredients together well with a wire whisk, mixer, or spoon. Cut chicken breasts into lengthwise strips or chunks. Place all of the chicken pieces in the sauce and stir well to coat. Place coating in a plastic bag, bowl or other container with a lid. Place about one pound of chicken (or 1/2 a single recipe) in the crumb mixture. Seal container and shake well to coat pieces with crumbs. Place chicken on spray-treated or greased baking sheets and bake at 375° for 15-20 minutes, turning once. Remove from oven and cool on baking sheets.

Freezing and Cooking Directions:

When cool, place trays of fingers or chunks in freezer and freeze until firm. Place frozen fingers or chunks in freezer ziptop bag or rigid container.

To serve, place frozen fingers or chunks on a baking sheet and reheat at 400° for 5-10 minutes until sizzling and hot.

Comments:

These have so many great uses! Our kids love them. To make them lower in fat, use skim milk, fat free mayonnaise, and diet ranch dressing. You'll never miss the fat!

30 DAY GOURMET
PORK/FISH ENTREES

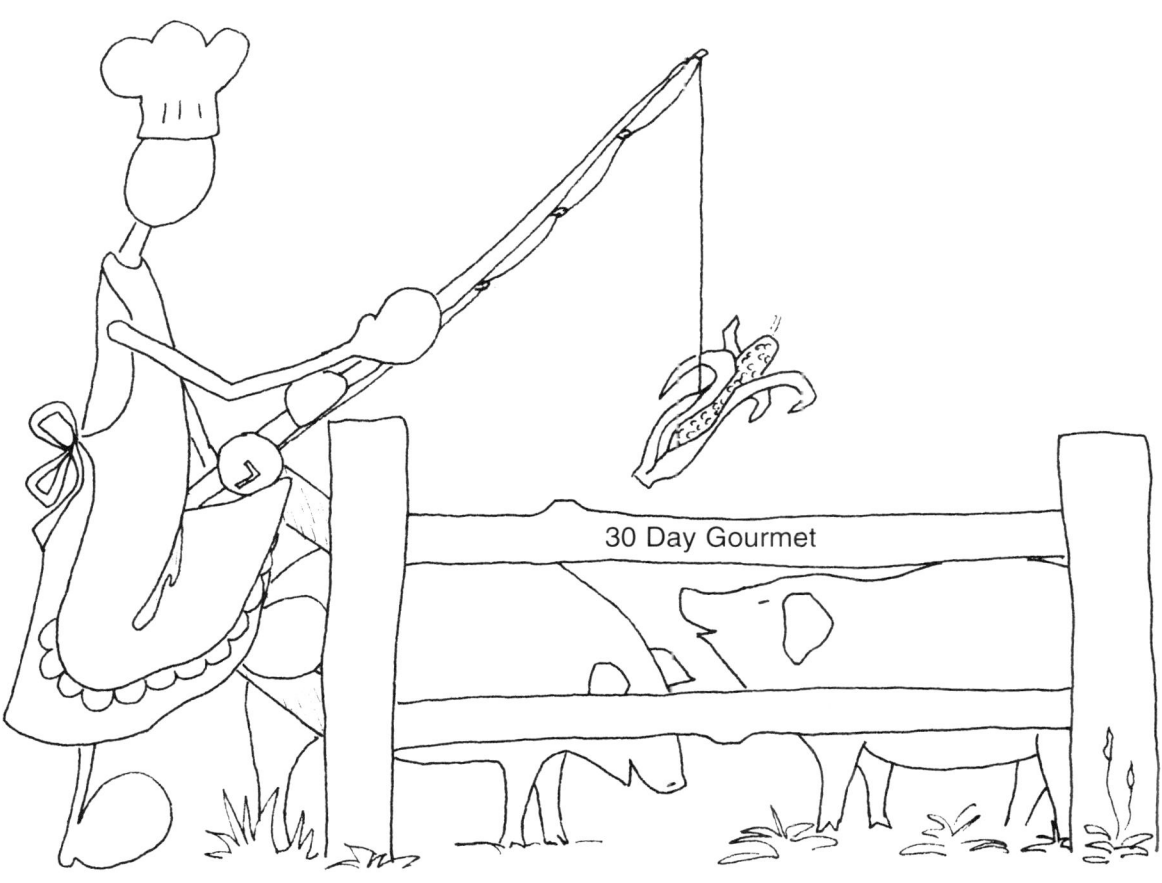

30 Day Gourmet

- ❖ Ham Loaf/Ham Balls
- ❖ Ham Sauces
- ❖ Ham & Potato Casserole
- ❖ Crock Pot Pork Barbecues
- ❖ Marinade for Pork
- ❖ Sausage Rice Bake
- ❖ Mexican Pork Chops
- ❖ Breaded Fish Fillets
- ❖ West Country Cod
- ❖ Citrus Marinade for Fish

TIPS FOR PORK & FISH ENTREES

T.	= Tablespoon
t.	= teaspoon
C.	= Cup
lb.	= pound
oz.	= ounce

As always, if you have any questions, please call, write, or e-mail us. We will try to get an answer to you as soon as possible.
Phone: 1-800-9-MANUAL
e-mail: office@30daygourmet.com

☑ Most fresh fish should not have a strong "fishy" odor and the packages should not be leaking into each other.

☑ 1/4 lb. of raw fish is an adult serving.

☑ 1/2 C. of cooked ground pork (as in sausage), is an adult serving.

☑ Cured pork products like ham and bacon should only be frozen for a month, or they will develop a strong flavor.

☑ You can grind your own ham in a food processor or ask your butcher to do it. When doing it yourself, cut the ham into 2" cubes and use the chopping blade. Pulse the blade until it is evenly ground. Experiment with textures.

☛Healthy Tips☚

We hope that you will find the recipes in this pack to be nutritious, tasty, simple and completely freezable. We are not dietitians, but by way of our own fat-reducing, nutrition-lifting journey, have gained some knowledge and practical application in serving great tasting and good-for-you foods. In all of the following recipes, feel free to substitute lower fat or fat free products wherever you choose.

♦ Broil, bake, or grill fish instead of frying it in fat.

♦ People tend to overcook both fish and pork cuts for fear of food poisoning. As soon as the fish is opaque and flakes easily, it is done. As soon as a pork cut is no longer pink in the center of the thickest part, it is done.

♦ To cut down on the fat in ground pork, ask the butcher to mix in an equal quantity of ground turkey.

Recipe: Ham Loaf/ Ham Balls

Meals:	1	2	3	4	5	6
serves 4-6						

Ingredients:

	1	2	3	4	5	6
ground ham, cooked	1 1/2 lbs.	3 lbs.	4 1/2 lbs.	6 lbs.	7 1/2 lbs.	9 lbs.
lean ground beef, uncooked	3/4 lbs.	1 1/2 lbs.	2 1/4 lbs.	3 lbs.	3 3/4 lbs.	4 1/2 lbs.
eggs	2	4	6	8	10	12
prepared mustard	2 t.	1 T.+1 t.	2 T.	2T.+2t.	3 T.+1 t.	1/4 C.
salt	1/2 t.	1 t.	1 1/2 t.	2 t.	2 1/2 t.	1 T.
milk	1 C.	2 C.	3 C.	4 C.	5 C.	6 C.
fine soda cracker crumbs	3/4 C.	1 1/2 C.	2 1/4 C.	3 C.	3 3/4 C.	4 1/2 C.

Containers: gallon freezer bags or loaf pans

Assembly Directions:
Combine all the ingredients in a large bowl. Mix very well with your hands (If you don't like the thought of that, use rubber or disposable gloves.)

Freezing and Cooking Directions:
Place the mixture in one gallon freezer bags or in 9x5x3 loaf pans, well wrapped. Label and freeze. Freezing guidelines recommend that you do not freeze ham for longer than 1 month.
To serve, thaw. Remove from freezer bag (if necessary) and shape into loaf in 9x5x3 pan. Cover pan with foil. Bake at 325° for a total of 75 minutes. While the loaf is baking, prepare one of the *optional sauces.
After 30 minutes of baking time, add the sauce. Baste every 10-15 minutes till done.

Ham Balls: For ham balls, just shape the mixture into walnut sized balls. We use a cookie scoop for quicker and more uniform ham balls. Bake 45 minutes at 350°, adding sauce after 15 minutes.

Comments:
As with most of our recipes, you may bake the entree on assembly day, cool and freeze or you may freeze it uncooked and do it later. Your choice generally depends on how much prep time you have each day.

*See Optional Sauces for Ham Loaf and Ham Balls in *Pork Entrees*.

OPTIONAL SAUCES FOR HAM LOAF & HAM BALLS

For each of these sauces, mix all the ingredients together. Add to the ham loaf after 30 minutes of baking time. Baste the meat with the sauce every 10 minutes after that. Add to the ham balls after 15 minutes of baking time. Pass any extra sauce with the meat at the table. Both the loaf and the ham balls may be fully cooked with the sauce and then frozen together for a quicker warm up time before serving.

HAM SAUCE 1:

1 3/4 C. brown sugar
1 T. water

2 t. prepared mustard
1 T. vinegar

HAM SAUCE 2:

1 C. brown sugar
2 t. dry mustard

1/4 C. maple syrup or honey
1 small can of crushed pineapple, drained

HAM SAUCE 3:

16 oz. can whole cranberry sauce
1 T. prepared mustard
1 1/2 t. vinegar

HAM SAUCE 4:

1/2 C. raisins
1 t. dry mustard
2 T. molasses
1/4 C. water

3 T. flour
3 T. vinegar
1 T. beef bouillon granules
(3 cubes, crushed)

HAM SAUCE 5:

1 C. currant jelly

2 T. prepared mustard

HAM SAUCE 6:

1/4 C. apricot jam
2 t. dijon-type mustard

2 t. vinegar

HAM SAUCE 7:

1/2 C. water (or pineapple juice)
1 T. cornstarch
1 T. soy sauce
1/4 C. vinegar

1 T. ketchup
1/4 C. sugar

HAM SAUCE 8:

3/4-1 C. of any barbecue sauce

HAM SAUCE 9:

3/4 C. pineapple juice
1/3 C. soy sauce

1 T. cornstarch
3 T. honey

Recipe: Ham & Potato Casserole/Scalloped Potatoes

Meals: serves 6-8	1	2	3	4	5	6
Ingredients:						
hash browns;frozen,cubed	2 lbs.	4 lbs.	6 lbs.	8 lbs.	10 lbs.	12 lbs.
*white sauce	1 1/2 C.	3 C.	4 1/2 C.	6 C.	7 1/2 C.	9 C.
butter/margarine, melted	2 T.	4 T.	6 T.	8 T.	10 T.	12 T.
sour cream	16 oz.	32 oz.	48 oz.	64 oz.	80 oz.	96 oz.
cooked ham, cubed	2 C.	4 C.	6 C.	8 C.	10 C.	12 C.
pepper	1/2 t.	1 t.	1 1/2 t.	2 t.	2 1/2 t.	1 T.
green onion, chopped	1/3 C.	2/3 C.	1 C.	1 1/3 C.	1 2/3 C.	2 C.
cheddar cheese, shredded	1 C. (4 oz.)	2 C. (8 oz.)	3 C. (12 oz.)	4 C. (16 oz.)	5 C. (20 oz.)	6 C. (24 oz.)
corn flakes, crushed	2 C.	4 C.	6 C.	8 C.	10 C.	12 C.
margarine, melted	1/4 C.	1/2 C.	3/4 C.	1 C.	1 1/4 C.	1 1/2 C.

Containers: gallon freezer bags, rigid freezer containers or 9x13 pans
Assembly Directions:
Combine first 8 ingredients and mix well. Place this mixture in a 9x13 pan, two smaller pans, ziptop bags or other freezer containers. Combine corn flake crumbs and margarine/butter. Sprinkle these over pans or place in separate ziptop bags.
For Scalloped Potatoes: Omit ham and assemble the same.

Freezing and Cooking Directions:
Cover casserole tightly with foil, freezer wrap or place pan in 2 gallon ziptop freezer bag. Seal bags well, squeezing out excess air. Label and freeze.
To serve, thaw completely. If necessary, sprinkle with cornflake topping. Bake at 350° for 1 hour.
Frozen casserole may be baked for 1 1/2 hours at 350°.
Comments:
Be sure to freeze the bag of crumbs WITH the casserole or you will lose them! And yes, it is best to do the crumb topping now. Murphy's Law says those corn flakes will never be there the day you need them, you know!
Mixing this in a LARGE pot or plastic tub with your hands is the quickest but you may get frostbite! Wear thick rubber gloves. They work great!
For a lower fat meal, use our fat free white sauce along with lower or fat free sour cream and cheese.
*See White Sauce recipe in Side Dishes.

Recipe: Crock Pot Pork Barbecues

Meals: serves 4-6	1	2	3	4	5	6
Ingredients:						
onion, chopped	1/2 C.	1 C.	1 1/2 C.	2 C.	2 1/2 C.	3 C.
celery, chopped	1/4 C.	1/2 C.	3/4 C.	1 C.	1 1/4 C.	1 1/2 C.
ketchup	1/2 C.	1 C.	1 1/2 C.	2 C.	2 1/2 C.	3 C.
water	1/3 C.	2/3 C.	1 C.	1 1/3 C.	1 2/3 C.	2 C.
lemon juice	2 T.	1/4 C.	1/4 C.+2 T.	1/2 C.	1/2 C.+2 T.	3/4 C.
brown sugar or molasses	1 T.	2 T.	3 T.	1/4 C.	1/4 C.+1 T.	1/4 C.+2 T.
Worcestershire sauce	1 T.	2 T.	3 T.	1/4 C.	1/4 C.+1 T.	1/4 C.+2 T.
vinegar	1 T.	2 T.	3 T.	1/4 C.	1/4 C.+1 T.	1/4 C.+2 T.
prepared mustard	1 T.	2 T.	3 T.	1/4 C.	1/4 C.+1 T.	1/4 C.+2 T.
salt and pepper to taste						
pork roast	1 1/2 lb.	3 lb.	4 1/2 lb.	6 lb.	7 1/2 lb.	9 lb.

On Hand: hoagie rolls or sandwich buns

Containers: gallon freezer bags or rigid containers suitable for your family

Assembly Directions:
In crock pot, stir all ingredients together except the meat. Set the meat on top of the sauce and simmer until meat is easily shredded with a fork. Simmer 6-8 hours or overnight. Shred the meat while it is warm. Stir in the sauce well Cool.

Freezing and Cooking Directions:
When the meat is cool, portion it into freezer bags or rigid containers. Seal, label, and freeze.
To serve, thaw. Heat the meat in the microwave, in a saucepan on low, or in the oven at 350° until hot (15-20 minutes per recipe).
Options:*Add a few drops of liquid smoke for a smoky flavor.
    ***Diced bell peppers may be added to the sauce ingredients: 1/2-1 C. pepper per recipe.**

Recipe: Marinade for Pork

Meals: serves 4	**1**	**2**	**3**	**4**	**5**	**6**
Ingredients:						
pork chops	6-8	12-16	18-24	24-32	30-40	36-48
Marinade:						
pineapple juice	16 oz.	32 oz.	48 oz.	64 oz.	80 oz.	96 oz.
*soy sauce (lite &/or reduced salt works fine)	1/2 C.	1 C.	1 1/2 C.	2 C.	2 1/2 C.	3 C.
ginger, ground	1 t.	2 t.	1 T.	1 T.+ 1 t.	1 T.+ 2 t.	2 T.
garlic, minced	1/2 t.	1 t.	1 1/2 t.	2 t.	2 1/2 t.	1 T.
italian dressing (diet is fine)	1/3 C.	2/3 C.	1 C.	1 1/3 C.	1 2/3 C.	2 C.

Containers: gallon freezer bags or rigid containers suitable for your family

Assembly Directions:
Combine all marinade ingredients. Place meat in freezer bags or containers. Pour marinade over meat. (Each meal makes approximately 3 cups.)

Freezing and Cooking Directions:
Label and freeze.
To serve, thaw. Grill or cook pork. Discard marinade.

Comments:
*We usually buy our soy sauce at a restaurant supply store where it is MUCH cheaper!

Recipe: Sausage Rice Bake

Meals: serves 4-6	1	2	3	4	5	6
Ingredients:						
onion, minced	1/2 C.	1 C.	1 1/2 C.	2 C.	2 1/2 C.	3 C.
bulk turkey sausage	1/2 lb.	1 lb.	1 1/2 lb.	2 lb.	2 1/2 lb.	3 lb.
olive oil	3 T.	6 T.	1/2 C.+ 1 T.	3/4 C.	3/4 C.+ 3 T.	1 C.+2 T.
frozen peas (or any cooked/blanched veggie)	8 oz.	16 oz.	24 oz.	32 oz.	40 oz.	48 oz.
sliced mushrooms	4 1/2 oz.	9 oz.	13 1/2 oz.	18 oz.	22 1/2 oz.	27 oz.
beef broth	3/4 C.	1 1/2 C.	2 1/4 C.	3 C.	3 3/4 C.	4 1/2 C.
instant brown rice, uncooked	2 C.	4 C.	6 C.	8 C.	10 C.	12 C.
beef broth	1 1/2 C.	3 C.	4 1/2 C.	6 C.	7 1/2 C.	9 C.

On Hand: parmesan cheese, artichokes (optional) and sliced olives (optional)
Containers: gallon freezer bags or 8x8 casserole

Assembly Directions:
Saute minced onions and turkey sausage in olive oil until browned. Add frozen peas (or other cooked vegetable), mushrooms and beef broth. Simmer 10 minutes. Stir in uncooked rice and broth. Toss lightly and cool. (It will absorb the broth.)

Freezing and Cooking Directions:
Divide into suitable portions. Seal, label and freeze.
To serve, thaw freezer bag or casserole. Stir in 1/2 C. water for each meal.
If in bag, turn into sprayed 8x8 casserole. Sprinkle top with grated parmesan cheese. Bake at 375° for 20-30 minutes until rice is done.

Comments:
Using turkey sausage will keep this recipe the lowest in fat but any kind of sausage will work. Watch the "hotness" of the meat.
Options: Marinated artichokes or sliced olives are very good stirred into this dish. Keep them on hand and stir in just before topping with parmesan cheese.

Recipe: Mexican Pork Chops

Meals:	1	2	3	4	5	6
serves 4						
Ingredients:						
pork chops	6	12	18	24	30	36
vegetable oil	2 T.	1/4 C.	1/4 C.+2 T.	1/2 C.	1/2 C.+ 2T.	3/4 C.
water	1 1/2 C.	3 C.	4 1/2 C.	6 C.	7 1/2 C.	9 C.
long grain rice, uncooked	3/4 C.	1 1/2 C.	2 1/4 C.	3 C.	3 3/4 C.	4 1/2 C.
tomato sauce	8 oz.	16 oz.	24 oz.	32 oz.	40 oz.	48 oz.
taco seasoning mix	2 T.	1 packet	6 T.	2 packets	1/2 C.+2T.	3 packets
green pepper, chopped	1 med.	2 med.	3 med	4 med.	5 med.	6 med.
cheddar cheese, shredded	1 C. (4 oz.)	2 C. (8 oz.)	3 C. (12 oz.)	4 C. (16 oz.)	5 C. (20 oz.)	6 C. (24 oz.)

Containers: gallon freezer bags or 9x13 casserole

Assembly Directions:
To Pre-Bake on Cooking Day:
Brown the pork chops in a large skilled with the oil. Sprinkle them with salt and pepper(optional). In a sprayed 9x13 baking dish, combine the water, rice, tomato sauce and taco seasoning; mix well. Arrange the browned chops over the rice and top with green pepper. Cover and bake at 350° for 1 hour.
To Bake on Serving Day:
Brown FRESH pork chops in the oil. Cool and place in freezer container or bag. In a separate freezer ziptop bag or container, place rice, water, tomato sauce and taco seasoning. Stir well in container and seal. Seal cheese and pepper in separate bags. Label all bags and freeze.

Freezing and Cooking Directions:
Pre-Baked Casserole:
Remove from oven and cool. Wrap dish in freezer paper, or foil, or place dish in 2 gallon ziptop freezer bag. Put shredded cheese in a small ziptop bag and attach to the casserole dish. Seal, label, and freeze.
To serve, thaw casserole. Bake at 350° for 15 minutes. Sprinkle cheese and return to oven for 15 minutes.
Non-Baked Meal:
Tape all freezer bags together or put all in large 2 gallon ziptop bag.
To serve, thaw all bags. Pour contents of rice bag in sprayed 9x13 casserole. Arrange chops over rice. Sprinkle pepper over chops. Bake at 350° for 1 hour. Top with cheese and bake an additional 15 minutes.

Recipe: Breaded Fish Fillets

Meals: serves 4-6	1	2	3	4	5	6
Ingredients:						
fresh fish fillets	1 1/2 lbs.	3 lbs.	4 1/2 lbs.	6 lbs.	7 1/2 lbs.	9 lbs.
eggs	1	2	3	4	5	6
milk	1 T.	2 T.	3 T.	1/4 C.	1/4 C.+1 T.	1/4 C.+2T.
fresh bread crumbs	1 C.	2 C.	3 C.	4 C.	5 C.	6 C.
salt	1/2 t.	1 t.	1 1/2 t.	2 t.	2 1/2 t.	1 T.
pepper	1/4 t.	1/2 t.	3/4 t.	1 t.	1 1/4 t.	1 1/2 t.

Containers: gallon freezer bags or rigid containers suitable for your family

Assembly Directions:
Mix egg and milk together in a shallow bowl. In another bowl combine crumbs, salt, and pepper. Dip fish in egg mixture then dredge in crumbs on both sides.

Freezing and Cooking Directions:
Place fish on a cake cooling rack that is set on a cookie sheet. Place baking sheet with cooling rack and coated fish in freezer. Freeze until firm. Place fish in a single layer in a freezer container or gallon ziptop freezer bag. Label and put in freezer.
To serve, place frozen fish in a single layer on a sprayed or greased baking sheet. Bake 10 minutes at 450° or until opaque and flakes easily.

Recipe: West Country Cod

Meals:	1	2	3	4	5	6
serves 4-6						

Ingredients:

	1	2	3	4	5	6
white fish pieces	1 1/2 lbs.	3 lbs.	4 1/2 lbs.	6 lbs.	7 1/2 lbs.	9 lbs.
onion, chopped	1/2 C.	1 C.	1 1/2 C.	2 C.	2 1/2 C.	3 C.
butter/margarine	2 T.	1/4 C.	6 T.	1/2 C.	1/2 C.+2T.	3/4 C.
cornstarch	3 T.	3/8 C.	1/2 C.-1 T.	3/4 C.	3/4 C.+3T.	1 C.+ 2T.
white cooking wine or apple juice	2 C.	4 C.	6 C.	8 C.	10 C.	12 C.
Dijon-type mustard	1 t.	2 t.	1 T.	1 T.+1 t.	1 T.+ 2 t.	2 T.
dried parsley	1 T.	2 T.	3 T.	1/4 C.	1/4 C.+1 T.	1/4 C.+ 2T.

brown sugar to taste
salt and pepper to taste

Containers: quart ziptop freezer bags or 8x8 casserole

Assembly Directions:

To Pre-Bake:
Roll up each fillet (if possible) and arrange in a sprayed baking dish. Sprinkle the chopped onion over the fish.
Melt butter/margarine in a saucepan. Stir in the cornstarch and cook for one minute, stirring constantly.
Gradually stir in the juice or wine, mustard, parsley, brown sugar and seasoning. Bring to a boil,
stirring constantly. Remove from heat and pour sauce over fillets. Bake fish at 375° for 10-15 minutes.

To Bake on serving day:
Leave fish frozen or if purchased fresh, freeze in ziptop bags. Bag chopped onion. Prepare sauce as directed. Cool.
Place sauce in freezer bag or container.

Freezing and Cooking Directions:

For Pre-Baked Casserole:
Cool, wrap in freezer paper, foil, or place in 2 gallon ziptop bag. Label and freeze.
To serve, unwrap and thaw. Cover and bake at 375° until heated through (35-45 minutes). Taste and
adjust seasoning.

For Ziptop Fish and Sauce:
Leave fish frozen or if purchased fresh, freeze in ziptop bags. Cool sauce and put in quart sized ziptop bag.
Put fish, sauce and onion inside a large ziptop. Label and freeze.
To serve, thaw fish and sauce. Roll each fillet (if possible) and arrange in a sprayed baking dish. Sprinkle the
chopped onion over the fish. Pour sauce over fillets. Bake fish at 375° until heated through (35-45 minutes).
Taste and adjust seasonings.

Recipe: Citrus Marinade for Fish Fillets

Meals: serves 4-6	1	2	3	4	5	6
Ingredients: fish fillets	1 1/2 lbs.	3 lbs.	4 1/2 lbs.	6 lbs.	7 1/2 lbs.	9 lbs.
Marinade: lime juice	1/3 C.	2/3 C.	1 C.	1 1/3 C.	1 2/3 C.	2 C.
cooking oil	1 T.	2 T.	3 T.	1/4 C.	1/4 C.+1 T.	1/4 C.+ 2T.
salt	1/4 t.	1/2 t.	3/4 t.	1 t.	1 1/4 t.	1 1/2 t.
water	1/3 C.	2/3 C.	1 C.	1 1/3 C.	1 2/3 C.	2 C.
honey (optional)	1 T.	2 T.	3 T.	1/4 C.	1/4 C.+1 T.	1/4 C.+ 2T.
dill weed, dried	1/2 t.	1 t.	1 1/2 t.	2 t.	2 1/2 t.	1 T.

Containers: ziptop freezer bags or rigid containers.

Assembly Directions:
Combine marinade ingredients.

Freezing and Cooking Directions:
Pour marinade into equal ziptop bags or freezer containers. (Each meal equals approximately 3/4 C. marinade.) Add
fillets to marinade. Seal, label and freeze.
To serve, thaw in marinade until completely softened. Remove fish from marinade, reserving it for later. Place on
greased broiler rack or grill. Tuck under any thin portion. Broil 4" from heat element, basting often with reserved
marinade, until fish flakes easily. It takes just a few minutes, so watch carefully. Brush with marinade again
just before serving. Discard any leftover marinade.

30 DAY GOURMET
SIDE DISHES/MISC.

❖ Cheese-Filled Shells
❖ Wild Rice Dressing
❖ Quiche in a Bag
❖ Fruit Slush
❖ Mexicali Casserole
❖ California Pilaf

❖ Tara's Macaroni & Cheese
❖ Make Ahead Mashed Potatoes
❖ Gramette's Dressing
❖ Crispy, Cheesy Potatoes
❖ Pasta w/Veggies & Herb Sauce
❖ Champagne Salad

Sauces:
❖ White Sauce
❖ Fat Free White Sauce

TIPS FOR SIDES, SALADS, MISC.

T. = Tablespoon t. = teaspoon C. = Cup lb. = pound oz. = ounce	As always, if you have any questions, please call, write, or e-mail us. We will try to get an answer to you as soon as possible. Phone: 1-800-9-MANUAL e-mail: office@30daygourmet.com

☑ Meats may be added to many of these dishes if you want to use them as a main dish:

> Cooked ground beef or sausage may be added to the *Cheese Stuffed Shells*.
> Meat included in the *Mexicali Casserole* would make a great main dish.
> The sausage may be increased in the *Wild Rice Dressing*.
> *Quiche in a Bag* could easily have sausage or ham added to it.
> Ham could also be included in the *Macaroni and Cheese*.

☑ Many of these side dishes can be used as festive holiday dishes. Wouldn't it be great to have them ready in the freezer ahead of time?

☑ The *Make Ahead Mashed Potatoes* also serve as a good top layer to many casseroles and thick stews.

☑ Many of these recipes make great, convenient picnic or pot luck supper foods.

☑ All fresh vegetables except chopped onion, chopped green pepper, and chopped celery must be blanched before being added to foods going into the freezer. See the *Appendix* section for a Vegetable Blanching Chart.

☑ 1 lb. of fresh vegetables with little waste (green beans, for example) or 2 lbs. with shells or heavy peels (peas, beets, winter squash, for example) serves 3-4 adults.

☑ A 16 oz. can or 10 oz. of frozen vegetables serves 3-4 adults.

☛Healthy Tips☚

♦ *Making these dishes ahead really helps to plan your "5 a day" servings of fruits and veggies.*

♦ *If you plan a potato side dish for your dinners, a good vegetable salad and one other raw or cooked vegetable plus a frozen fruit salad for dessert, you will have had four of those servings.*

♦ *Several of these recipes make good meatless main dishes.*

♦ *We use whole wheat pastas, breads, and brown rice when assembling these recipes. This helps tremendously in getting enough fiber into our diets.*

Recipe: Cheese-Filled Shells

Meals: serves 6-8 Ingredients:	40 shells	80 shells	120 shells	160 shells	200 shells	240 shells
jumbo shells	40 (12 oz. box)	80 (24 oz.)	120 (36 oz.)	160 (48 oz.)	200 (60 oz.)	240 (72 oz.)
cottage cheese	32 oz.	64 oz.	96 oz.	128 oz.	160 oz.	192 oz.
shredded mozzarella cheese	16 oz.	32 oz.	48 oz.	64 oz.	80 oz.	96 oz.
grated parmesan cheese	3/4 C.	1 1/2 C.	2 1/4 C.	3 C.	3 3/4 C.	4 1/2 C.
eggs	3	6	9	12	15	18
oregano	3/4 t.	1 1/2 t.	2 1/4 t.	1 T.	1 T.+3/4 t.	1 T.+1 1/2t
salt (optional)	1/2 t.	1 t.	1 1/2 t.	2 t.	2 1/2 t.	1 T.
pepper	1/2 t.	1 t.	1 1/2 t.	2 t.	2 1/2 t.	1 T.
On Hand: *spaghetti sauce	28 oz. (3 1/2 C.)	56 oz. (7 C.)	84 oz. (10 1/2 C.)	112 oz. (14 C.)	140 oz. (17 1/2 C.)	168 oz. (21 C.)

Containers: rigid containers for shells, freezer ziptops for homemade sauce

Assembly Directions:
Cook jumbo shells 1/2 of recommended time until just limp. Drain. Cool in a single layer on pan or waxed paper
Combine cheeses, eggs, oregano, salt and pepper. Fill each shell with 2 T. cheese mixture. *Tip: Using an icing bag with a wide tip works well for this or make your own by snipping the corner off a freezer bag.*

Freezing and Cooking Directions:
Freeze quantity of shells for one meal in a rigid container. Freeze homemade sauce in ziptop bag.
To serve, thaw cheese-filled shells and sauce. Spread 1/2 C. spaghetti sauce in bottom of 9x13 baking dish. Arrange shells in dish. Pour remaining sauce over shells. Warm at 350° for 30 minutes.

Comments:
Our kids really like these. They can be totally fat free or lower in fat depending upon your cheese sauce, and egg choices. One recipe makes a lot, so you might divide it into two meals or one meal and a few lunches like we do.

We buy whole wheat shells through our food co-op. You could also use manicotti shells.
See our Spaghetti Sauce recipe in Beef Entrees. You can leave out the meat if you want a meatless dish.

Recipe: Wild Rice Dressing (with sausage added, it's a main dish!)

Meals:	1	2	3	4	5	6
serves 4-6						
Ingredients:						
*mild pork or turkey sausage (optional)	1/2 lb.	1 lb.	1 1/2 lb.	2 lb.	2 1/2 lb.	3 lb.
wild rice, cooked (dry)	2 C. (1/2 C.)	4 C. (1 C.)	6 C. (1 1/2 C.)	8 C. (2 C.)	10 C. (2 1/2 C.)	12 C. (3 C.)
celery, diced or sliced	1 C.	2 C.	3 C.	4 C.	5 C.	6 C.
onion, diced	1 C.	2 C.	3 C.	4 C.	5 C.	6 C.
poultry seasoning	1 T.	2 T.	3 T.	1/4 C.	1/4 C.+1 T.	1/4 C.+2T.
turkey or chicken broth	1 C.	2 C.	3 C.	4 C.	5 C.	6 C.
brown sugar or molasses	1 T.	2 T.	3 T.	1/4 C.	1/4 C.+1 T.	1/4 C.+2T.
parsley flakes	1 T.	2 T.	3 T.	1/4 C.	1/4 C.+1 T.	1/4 C.+2T.
cranberries, chopped (fresh or frozen)	1/2 C.	1 C.	1 1/2 C.	2 C.	2 1/2 C.	3 C.
green apples, chopped	2 C.	4 C.	6 C.	8 C.	10 C.	12 C.
pecans or walnuts, chopped	3/4 C.	1 1/2 C.	2 1/4 C.	3 C.	3 3/4 C.	4 1/2 C.
wheat or white bread cubes, stale or dry	5 C.	10 C.	15 C.	20 C.	25 C.	30 C.

Containers: gallon freezer ziptop bags or rigid containers

Assembly Directions:
Cook and crumble pork or turkey sausage. Cook wild rice (thoroughly, this time!). In a skillet, saute the celery, onion, and poultry seasoning (this may be steam-sauteed in the microwave) until crisp tender. Add broth and brown sugar or molasses to celery mixture. Mix well. Add sausage (opt.), parsley flakes, cranberries, apples, nuts, bread cubes and rice. Mix well.

Freezing and Cooking Directions:
Place mixture in freezer ziptops or rigid containers. Label and freeze.
To serve, thaw completely and transfer dressing to a spray-treated or greased baking dish. Cover and bake at 350^C for 45 minutes. Uncover and bake an additional 15 minutes.

Comments:
Great to have this made and frozen for holiday or "special" meals. This dressing may be baked outside the bird or stuffed inside.
*Adding the sausage makes this a filling main dish entree.

Recipe: Quiche in a Bag

Meals:	1	2	3	4	5	6
serves 4-6						

Ingredients:

	1	2	3	4	5	6
*meat, cooked (any meat diced or browned and crumbled)	1 C.	2 C.	3 C.	4 C.	5 C.	6 C.
vegetable (any *raw, blanched; thawed frozen; or canned, drained)	3/4 C.	1 1/2 C.	2 1/4 C.	3 C.	3 3/4 C.	4 1/2 C.
cheddar cheese, shredded	1 C.	2 C.	3 C.	4 C.	5 C.	6 C.
onion, diced	1/4 C.	1/2 C.	3/4 C.	1 C.	1 1/4 C.	1 1/2 C.
milk	2 C.	4 C.	6 C.	8 C.	10 C.	12 C.
eggs	4	8	12	16	20	24
Tabasco sauce	1/8 t.	1/4 t.	3/8 t.	1/2 t.	1/2t.+1/8t.	3/4 t.
flour (whole wheat works fine)	1/2 C.	1 C.	1 1/2 C.	2 C.	2 1/2 C.	3 C.
baking powder	2 t.	1 T.+1 t.	2 T.	2 T.+2 t.	3 T.+1 t.	1/4 C.

Containers: gallon freezer ziptop bags

Assembly Directions:

Combine meat, vegetable, cheese, and onion. Place this mixture in a gallon ziptop bag or rigid freezer container
With a mixer or blender, combine the milk, eggs, Tabasco sauce, flour and baking powder. Pour into the bag with
the meat/vegetable mixture.

Freezing and Cooking Directions:

Seal, label, and freeze. To serve, thaw completely. Shake sealed container or bag well and pour into a spray-treated
or greased deep dish pie plate or quiche pan. Sprinkle with paprika if desired. Bake at 350° for 35-45 minutes,
until lightly browned on top and well set in the center. Cool about 5 minutes before serving.

Comments:

*This is one of those dishes that you can get on the table when you haven't even looked in the freezer until 5:30 (like
Nanci usually doesn't!). Just thaw the bag in the microwave, pour it in a dish and pop it in the oven. Presto -
dinner!*

*For a vegetarian meal, just leave out the meat and increase the veggies by 1 C. for each recipe.
See our Blanching Chart in the Appendix Section if you are using fresh vegetables.

Recipe: Fruit Slush

Makes:	16 C.	32 C.	48 C.	64 C.	80 C.	96 C.
Ingredients:						
fruit cocktail, in syrup	40 oz.	80 oz.	120 oz.	160 oz.	200 oz.	240 oz.
strawberries; sliced, sweetened, frozen	10 oz.	20 oz.	30 oz.	40 oz.	50 oz.	60 oz.
orange juice concentrate, frozen	12 oz.	24 oz.	36 oz.	48 oz.	60 oz.	72 oz.
pineapple; crushed, in juice	20 oz.	40 oz.	60 oz.	80 oz.	100 oz.	120 oz.
bananas, diced	3	6	9	12	15	18

Containers: quart sized freezer ziptop bags, small rigid containers, or foil baking cups

Assembly Directions:
Partially thaw strawberries, so they can be separated. Mix all the ingredients together including all the juices from the canned and frozen fruits.

Freezing and Cooking Directions:
Pour into suitable containers for your family. Allow about 1/4-1/3 C. per child, 1/2 C. per adult. The leftovers have to be re-frozen, so make sure not to have too much leftover. Label and freeze.
To serve, thaw 10-15 minutes before needed - it should be slushy.

Comments:
Fresh fruits may be added to your liking. Small Styrofoam cups with lids may be purchased at restaurant supply stores. These work well for take out lunches. By lunchtime, they will be slushy and ready to eat!

Recipe: Mexicali Casserole

Meals:	1	2	3	4	5	6

serves 4-6
Ingredients:

onion, chopped	1 C.	2 C.	3 C.	4 C.	5 C.	6 C.
kidney beans, canned	16 oz.	32 oz.	48 oz.	64 oz.	80 oz.	96 oz.
white or brown rice, cooked 1/2 recommended time	2 C.	4 C.	6 C.	8 C.	10 C.	12 C.
tomatoes; diced or crushed, in liquid (not sauce)	28 oz.	56 oz.	84 oz.	112 oz.	140 oz.	168 oz.
corn, canned	15 oz.	30 oz.	45 oz.	60 oz.	75 oz.	90 oz.
OR						
corn, frozen	1 3/4 C.	3 1/2 C.	5 1/4 C.	7 C.	8 3/4 C.	10 1/2 C
pepper to taste						
cheese, shredded	2 C.	4 C.	6 C.	8 C.	10 C.	12 C.

Containers: freezer bags or containers suitable for your family

Assembly Directions:
Drain and reserve liquid from tomatoes. Drain water from canned corn. Drain kidney beans. Saute onion in a small amount of liquid from tomatoes. Add beans, cooked rice, tomatoes, and corn.

Freezing and Cooking Directions:
Pour into freezer ziptop bags or rigid containers. Place cheese in a separate freezer bag or container. Label both and freeze.
To serve, thaw both bags completely. Pour rice mixture into spray treated 2 quart casserole. Sprinkle with cheese. Bake at 350° for 30 minutes or until heated thoroughly.

Comments:
Optional: This dish could serve as a meatless main entree or 2 1/2 C. of cooked ground beef may be added to the casserole before freezing. It could then be used as a main dish.

Recipe: California Pilaf

Meals:	1	2	3	4	5	6
serves 6						
Ingredients:						
quick cooking brown rice, uncooked	2 C.	4 C.	6 C.	8 C.	10 C.	12 C.
celery, diced	1 C.	2 C.	3 C.	4 C.	5 C.	6 C.
onion, diced	1/2 C.	1 C.	1 1/2 C.	2 C.	2 1/2 C.	3 C.
spaghetti, uncooked and broken into 1" pieces	1/2 C.	1 C.	1 1/2 C.	2 C.	2 1/2 C.	3 C.
butter/margarine	1/4 C.	1/2 C.	3/4 C.	1 C.	1 1/4 C.	1 1/2 C.
chicken broth powder	2 T.	1/4 C.	1/4 C.+2 T.	1/2 C.	1/2 C.+2 T.	3/4 C.
OR						
bouillon granules	2 t.	1 T.+1 t.	2 T.	2 T.+2 t.	3 T.+1 t.	4 T.
parsley flakes	1 t.	2 t.	1 T.	1 T.+1 t.	1 T.+2 t.	2 T.
ground thyme	1/2 t.	1 t.	1 1/2 t.	2 t.	2 1/2 t.	1 T.
pepper	1/4 t.	1/2 t.	3/4 t.	1 t.	1 1/4 t.	1 1/2 t.
water	2 C.	4 C.	6 C.	8 C.	10 C.	12 C.

Containers: freezer bags or rigid containers suitable for your family

Assembly Directions:

In a large skillet, saute the rice, celery, onion, and broken pasta in the butter. Stir constantly until the rice and pasta are golden brown. Stir in the parsley flakes, ground thyme and pepper. Cool. Stir in bouillon granules.

Freezing and Cooking Directions:

Place cooled rice mixture in freezer bags or rigid containers. Seal, label and freeze.

To serve, thaw thoroughly. Place mixture in a saucepan or skillet with a lid. Stir in the water. Bring to a boil, then reduce heat to a simmer. Cover pan with a lid and cook for 10 minutes. Remove pan from heat and let stand for 10 minutes before serving.

Comments:

Options: *The water may be added and the pilaf fully cooked on assembly day. The pilaf could then be reheated quickly in the oven or microwave.*
*This dish could serve as a meatless main entree or 2 1/2 C. of cooked meat may be added for a standard entree.

Recipe: Tara's Macaroni and Cheese

Meals:	1	2	3	4	5	6

serves 4

Ingredients:

	1	2	3	4	5	6
macaroni, fully cooked	4 C.(cooked) (8-9 oz. dry)	8 C.	12 C.	16 C.	20 C.	24 C.
*white sauce	2 C.	4 C.	6 C.	8 C.	10 C.	12 C.
cream cheese, softened	4 oz.	8 oz.	12 oz.	16 oz.	20 oz.	24 oz.
sharp cheddar cheese, shredded	2 C.	4 C.	6 C.	8 C.	10 C.	12 C.
crackers, crushed or fresh bread crumbs	1/2 C.	1 C.	1 1/2 C.	2 C.	2 1/2 C.	3 C.

salt and pepper to taste

Containers: freezer bags, containers, or sprayed/greased casserole dishes suitable for your family

Assembly Directions:
Stir white sauce, a little at a time, into the softened cream cheese, removing any lumps as you stir. Mix in the shredded cheese and cooked macaroni. Salt and pepper to taste.

Freezing and Cooking Directions:
Label, and freeze in bags or rigid containers. Place crumbs in a small bag or container. Attach to macaroni and cheese. Seal, label and freeze.
To serve, thaw both bags or containers. Press macaroni mixture into greased or sprayed 1 1/2-2 qt. baking dish. Sprinkle crumbs over macaroni. Bake at 375° for about 30 minutes until the edges are bubbly.

Comments:
Frozen vegetables like broccoli, chopped asparagus, or carrots may be stirred in on assembly day.
Fresh vegetables, including: carrots, onions, mushrooms, or peppers may be stirred in on the day you serve the dish.

*See our white sauce in Side Dish/Misc.

Recipe: Make Ahead Mashed Potatoes

Makes:	7 C.	14 C.	21 C.	28 C.	35 C.	42 C.
Ingredients:						
potatoes	5 lbs.	10 lbs.	15 lbs.	20 lbs.	25 lbs.	30 lbs.
egg	1	2	3	4	5	6
garlic powder	1/2 t.	1 t.	1 1/2 t.	2 t.	2 1/2 t.	1 T.
butter/margarine, melted	3 T.	1/4 C.+2 T.	1/2 C.+1 T.	3/4 C.	3/4 C.+3 T.	1 C.+2 T.
salt	1 t.	2 t.	1 T.	1 T.+1 t.	1 T.+2 t.	2 T.
cream cheese	8 oz.	16 oz.	24 oz.	32 oz.	40 oz.	48 oz.
almonds, sliced (optional)	1/4 C.	1/2 C.	3/4 C.	1 C.	1 1/4 C.	1 1/2 C.

paprika for color

Containers: quart or gallon freezer bags or rigid freezer containers

Assembly Directions:
Peel and quarter potatoes. Place the potatoes in a saucepan and cover completely with water. Bring to a boil, then gently until tender. Drain well. In large bowl, combine potatoes, cream cheese, egg , garlic powder and salt. Mash well by hand or with an electric mixer. Spoon potatoes into spray-treated or greased 3 qt. casserole or 9x13 pan Drizzle or brush melted butter over potatoes. Sprinkle with almonds (optional) and paprika. Refrigerate for up to 2 days or label and freeze for later.

Freezing and Cooking Directions:
Label and freeze in freezer ziptops or rigid containers.
To serve, thaw completely. Bake at 375° for 30-40 minutes until the top is golden.

Comments:
You'll love having this side dish handy. Our kids really love these (minus the almonds, of course!). Husbands, too.
Options: *1/4 C. crumbled, crisp bacon may be stirred in for great flavor.
        Potatoes may also be topped with 1/2 C. shredded cheddar cheese.

Recipe: Gramette's Dressing

Meals:	1	2	3	4	5	6
serves 8-10						

Ingredients:

	1	2	3	4	5	6
butter/margarine	1/4 C.	1/2 C.	3/4 C.	1 C.	1 1/4 C.	1 1/2 C.
celery, chopped	1 C.	2 C.	3 C.	4 C.	5 C.	6 C.
onion, chopped	1 C.	2 C.	3 C.	4 C.	5 C.	6 C.
sage, rubbed (to taste)	2 T.	1/4 C.	1/4 C.+2 T.	1/2 C.	1/2 C.+2 T.	3/4 C.
egg	1	2	3	4	5	6
wheat bread and cornbread, stale or dried (homemade or purchased)	8 C.total	16 C.total	24 C.total	32 C.total	40 C.total	48 C.total
chicken or turkey broth	2-3 C.	4-6 C.	6-9 C.	8-12 C.	10-15 C.	12-18 C.

Containers: freezer bags or rigid containers suitable for your family

Assembly Directions:
Melt butter in a large skillet. Saute' onion and celery until tender in butter (this can be micro-steamed). Add the sage, then cool the mixture. Add the egg and mix well. Add cubed breads and toss until well coated. Gradually drizzle on the broth and toss until the dressing has reached a stage that it is a little soggier than you would want to see it on your plate (remember that some of the moisture will evaporate during baking).

Freezing and Cooking Directions:
Transfer dressing mixture to a freezer bag or rigid container. Seal, label, and freeze.
To serve, bake covered in a sprayed or greased pan at 350° for 30 minutes, then raise the heat to 400° and bake uncovered for an additional 15 minutes until it is browned to your liking.

Comments:
Wouldn't it be great to serve homemade stuffing more than twice a year? You can't beat Gramette's recipe!

*This dish could serve as a meatless main entree or 2 1/2 C. of cooked meat may be added for a standard entree.

Recipe: Crispy, Cheesy Potatoes

Meals:	1	2	3	4	5	6
serves 6-8						

Ingredients:

	1	2	3	4	5	6
hash browns; shredded, frozen	32 oz.	64 oz.	96 oz.	128 oz.	160 oz.	192 oz.
onion, chopped	1/4 C.	1/2 C.	3/4 C.	1 C.	1 1/4 C.	1 1/2 C.
sour cream	16 oz.	32 oz.	48 oz.	64 oz.	80 oz.	96 oz.
*white sauce, chicken flavored	1 1/2 C.	3 C.	4 1/2 C.	6 C.	7 1/2 C.	9 C.
cheddar cheese, shredded	1 1/2 C.	3 C.	4 1/2 C.	6 C.	7 1/2 C.	9 C.
corn flake cereal	2 C.	4 C.	6 C.	8 C.	10 C.	12 C.
butter/margarine, melted	1/3 C.	2/3 C.	1 C.	1 1/3 C.	1 2/3 C.	2 C.

Containers: gallon freezer bags, rigid freezer containers or 9x13 pans

Assembly Directions:
Thaw the potatoes just slightly and break them apart well. Mix the onion, sour cream, white sauce, and cheddar cheese. Stir in half of the potatoes and mix well. Stir in the remaining potatoes. In another bowl or pan, melt the butter. Stir the corn flakes into the melted butter.

Freezing and Cooking Directions:
Press the potato mixture into a sprayed 9x13 baking pan or place in freezer bags or rigid containers.
Wrap pans with freezer paper or freezer weight foil or slip pan into 2 gallon ziptop freezer bag and seal. Put the corn flake/butter mixture into a small freezer bag or container. Attach to the potato mixture.
Label both and freeze.
To serve, thaw potatoes and crumb topping. If frozen in bags or containers, put into a sprayed or greased 9x13 pan and top with the crumb mixture. Bake at 350° for 1 hour.

Comments:
Be sure to attach the crumbs to the bag somehow or you'll lose them! And yes, it is best to do the crumb topping now. Murphy's Law says those corn flakes will never be there the day you need them, you know!
Mixing this in a LARGE pot or plastic tub with you hands is the quickest but you may get frostbite! Wear thick rubber gloves. They work great!
For a lower fat meal, use our fat free white sauce along with lower or fat free sour cream and cheese.

*See White Sauce recipe in *Side Dishes/Misc.*

Recipe: Pasta with Vegetables and Herb Sauce

Meals:	1	2	3	4	5	6
(serves 4-6)						
Ingredients:						
Sauce:						
milk	1/4 C.	1/2 C.	3/4 C.	1 C.	1 1/4 C.	1 1/2 C.
grated parmesan cheese	1/4 C.	1/2 C.	3/4 C.	1 C.	1 1/4 C.	1 1/2 C.
ricotta cheese (lowfat OK)	1/4 C.	1/2 C.	3/4 C.	1 C.	1 1/4 C.	1 1/2 C.
fresh parsley, chopped	1/4 C.	1/2 C.	3/4 C.	1 C.	1 1/4 C.	1 1/2 C.
green onions, sliced	2	4	6	8	10	12
dried basil leaves	2 t.	1 T.+1 t.	2 T.	2 T.+2 t.	3 T.+1 t.	4 T.
garlic, minced	1/2 t.	1 t.	1 1/2 t.	2 t.	2 1/2 t.	1 T.
Pasta & Vegetables:						
water	3 qts.	6 qts.	9 qts.	12 qts.	15 qts.	18 qts.
fettucini or any pasta	4 oz.	8 oz.	12 oz.	16 oz.	20 oz.	24 oz.
carrots, sliced	2 C.	4 C.	6 C.	8 C.	10 C.	12 C.
broccoli florets	1 C.	2 C.	3 C.	4 C.	5 C.	6 C.
yellow squash, sliced	1 1/4 C.	2 1/2 C.	3 3/4 C.	5 C.	6 1/4 C.	7 1/2 C.
zucchini, sliced	1 1/4 C.	2 1/2 C.	3 3/4 C.	5 C.	6 1/4 C.	7 1/2 C.
snow peas	1/2 C.	1 C.	1 1/2 C.	2 C.	2 1/2 C.	3 C.

Containers: freezer bags or rigid containers suitable for your family

Assembly Directions:

Sauce: Puree the sauce ingredients together in a blender or food processor.
Pasta & Vegetables: Bring water to a boil. In the boiling water, cook the pasta and carrots together for 6 minutes. Add the broccoli and boil 2 minutes. Add both squashes and boil and additional 2 minutes. Add the snow peas just before draining. Drain pasta and vegetables.

Freezing and Cooking Directions:

Freeze vegetables and pasta together in a freezer bag or rigid container. Place sauce in a smaller container or bag and attach to pasta and vegetables. Label and freeze.
To serve, thaw both bags or containers thoroughly. Drop vegetable/pasta mix into boiling water briefly to re-heat. Drain and stir in thawed sauce.

Comments: You can use purchased frozen vegetables if you like, but don't boil them with the pasta. Place the cooked pasta in the freezer container and measure the frozen vegetables straight into the bag without thawing. To serve, boil the thawed ingredients as above, but boil until the vegetables have reached the desired tenderness.

Recipe: Champagne Salad

Makes:	8 C.	16 C.	24 C.	32 C.	40 C.	48 C.
Ingredients:						
sugar	3/4 C.	1 1/2 C.	2 1/4 C.	3 C.	3 3/4 C.	4 1/2 C.
light cream cheese (at room temperature)	8 oz.	16 oz.	24 oz.	32 oz.	40 oz.	48 oz.
frozen, sliced strawberries; thawed	10 oz.	20 oz.	30 oz.	40 oz.	50 oz.	60 oz.
canned, crushed pineapple	20 oz.	40 oz.	60 oz.	80 oz.	100 oz.	120 oz.
bananas, diced	2	4	6	8	10	12
walnuts or pecans, chopped (optional)	1 C.	2 C.	3 C.	4 C.	5 C.	6 C.
*frozen whipped topping, thawed	10 oz.	20 oz.	30 oz.	40 oz.	50 oz.	60 oz.

Containers: Rigid, plastic containers with lids, 9x13 or other metal or glass dishes that can be covered with foil or freezer wrap. This salad may also be frozen in cupcake liners and placed in a ziptop bag.

Assembly Directions:
Drain pineapple. In a large mixing container, cream the sugar and cream cheese together. Add strawberries, pineapple, bananas, and nuts (optional). Mix well. Fold in the whipped topping.

Freezing and Cooking Directions:
Spread in desired containers. Label and freeze.
To serve, thaw small portions 10-15 minutes before cutting into squares to serve, or large portions up to 30 minutes before serving.

Comments:
*4-5 Cups of real whipped cream may be substituted for the 10 oz. container of whipped topping.
*One recipe makes approximately 8 Cups of salad. Re-freeze leftovers.
*Try your own combinations of fruit. Even drained fruit cocktail, or melon balls would be good. Raspberries and blueberries work well because of their small size.
*If you want a less "sweet" salad, substitute 1 1/2 C. of sour cream for the whipped topping. (Fat free works very well.
*Our husbands love this and our kids mostly do ☺.

Recipe: White Sauce

Makes:	6 C.	12 C.	24 C.
Ingredients:			
butter/margarine or cooking oil (canola works fine)	3/4 C.	1 1/2 C.	3 C.
flour, (1/2 whole wheat is fine)	3/4 C.	1 1/2 C.	3 C.
milk	6 C.	12 C.	24 C.
chicken or beef flavoring:			
bouillon granules	2 T.	1/4 C.	1/2 C.
OR			
bouillon cubes	6	12	24
OR			
*broth powder	1/4 C.	1/2 C.	1 C.

Assembly Directions:

In a large, heavy bottomed or Teflon saucepan or stock pot, melt/warm the butter or oil over low heat. Add the flour and stir until the mixture is smooth. Cook the flour/oil mixture until it begins to bubble. Do NOT let it brown. Gradually add the milk, stirring CONSTANTLY. When the sauce has thickened (be patient; a 12-cup batch will take 30 minutes or so), stir in the bouillon granules, bouillon cubes, or the broth powder.

When making this sauce in more than 12-cup batches, it becomes difficult to keep from scorching it. We try to make 2 batches in different pans at once on different burners. It's a boring few hours of stirring (we usually make 60 cups each cooking day) but then it's all done and it is DELICIOUS!

Freezing and Cooking Directions:

When combined with other foods in casseroles, etc., this sauce freezes well. We would not recommend freezing it separately.

Comments:

We use this sauce or our Fat Free White Sauce any time white sauce is called for in one of our recipes. It is a great substitute for canned, creamed soups and saves money. If you use skim milk and canola oil, it is lower in fat and much better for your health, too. It can be seasoned with salt and pepper or other seasonings.

*To flavor our sauce, we always use a fat free, all natural broth powder (chicken or beef) that we order in bulk from our Food Co-operative. If you would like to order the broth powder directly from the company, you may

call or write: *Frontier Herbs*
Box 299
Norway, IA 52318
(319)227-7991

*1 1/2 C. of White Sauce = 1 small can (10 3/4 oz.) of soup.

Recipe: (Almost) Fat Free White Sauce

Makes:	6 C.	12 C.	24 C.
Ingredients:			
flour, (1/2 whole wheat is fine)	1 C.	2 C.	4 C.
skim milk	6 C.	12 C.	24 C.
chicken or beef flavoring:			
bouillon granules	2 T.	1/4 C.	1/2 C.
OR			
bouillon cubes	6	12	24
OR			
*broth powder	1/4 C.	1/2 C.	1 C.

Optional: For more flavor and vitamins, add any of these finely minced vegetables: Sauteed or steamed onion, celery, mushrooms, broccoli.

Optional: For a cheese sauce, just add shredded cheddar, Swiss or grated parmesan cheese in desired amounts while sauce is still hot. Stir until melted.

Assembly Directions:

In a saucepan, warm 2/3 of the total amount of skim milk. Place all of the flour and broth flavoring in a mixing bowl and gradually stir in the remaining 1/3 of the milk. When the milk/flour mixture is no longer lumpy, add it to the warm milk in the saucepan. Stirring constantly over medium, heat, bring the sauce to a gentle boil. Allow the sauce to boil one minute while continuing to stir. Remove saucepan from heat. Add any of the vegetable options.

Freezing and Cooking Directions:

When combined with other foods in casseroles, etc. this sauce freezes well. We would not recommend freezing it separately.

Comments:

We use this sauce or our White Sauce any time it is called for in one of our recipes. It is a great substitute for canned, creamed soups and saves money.

*To flavor our sauce we always use a fat free, all natural broth powder (chicken or beef) that we order in bulk from our Food Co-operative. If you would like to order the broth powder directly from the company, you may call or write: *Frontier Herbs*
Box 299
Norway, IA 52318
(319)227-7991

*We always make this a day or two before cooking day, as it is very time consuming. To store easily, cool sauce in a large roasting pan. Pour sauce (using a funnel) back into the plastic milk jugs and refrigerate.

*This recipe's fat content depends on the amount of fat in the milk you choose and whether or not you steam or saute any added vegetables in oil. Cheese, of course, will also add to the fat content.

*1 1/2 C. of White Sauce = 1 small can (10 3/4 oz.) of soup.

30 DAY GOURMET SNACKS/DESSERTS

- ❖ No-Bake Cookies
- ❖ Peanut Butter Balls
- ❖ Good-for-You Granola
- ❖ Breakfast McBiscuits
- ❖ Frozen Peanut Butter Bars

- ❖ Apple Squares
- ❖ Mozzarella Stix
- ❖ Snackin' Mix
- ❖ Stovetop Cereal Cookies
- ❖ Granola Bars

MASTER MIXES:
- ❖ Oatmeal Cookie Mix
- ❖ Master Baking Mix
- ❖ Quick Cobbler Mix

TIPS FOR SNACKS & DESSERTS

Kids- ya gotta love 'em! And we all do. But sometimes the best moms and dads get weary just trying to keep up with the little darlings. Whether your children are in the up-at-night infancy stage, the picky "I want my way" toddler time, the wannabe independent elementary grades, or the so-busy-you-rarely-see-'em teenage years, YOU ARE BUSY and THEY ARE HUNGRY!

Statistics about the health and eating habits of our children are not encouraging. Kids today exercise less and are much heavier than they used to be. High cholesterol and high blood pressure are not uncommon. The possible connections between many learning disabilities and the foods our children eat are being increasingly explored.

All the experts say that our children need to eat more fruit, vegetables, and fiber. We all want them to eat healthier, but how? The ready availability of snack foods and the bombardment of advertising promoting them to our children is at an all-time high. Most of these snacks, however, are of little nutritional value and are incredibly expensive. They also often help lay the groundwork for a lifetime of poor eating habits.

❖

So what's a parent to do? For us, part of the answer has come with bulk snack cooking. Like our 30 DAY GOURMET dinnertime planning, we have found that having snacks readily available in the freezer keeps us from "drive-thru" snacking and saves us lots of money. The recipes included here are some of our kids' (Katie, Estherre, Becky, Hannah, Adam, Lydia, and Jenna)favorites. We tested over 50 healthy snacks on them (and a few neighbor kids!) and these were the winners. We hope you enjoy them, too!

☛Healthy Tips☚

Natural Peanut Butter is much better for kids than the "regular unpronounceables". Natural peanut butter is just that - peanuts only (and maybe salt). Some grocery stores now carry it as well as food cooperatives. Other nut butters, such as cashew or almond, may be substituted.

Honey may be used for corn syrup in any recipe. Honey, however, has a stronger flavor, so you might buy the lightest color or clover honey which will be the mildest.

Unsweetened Apple Sauce in place of oil for baking is often a good substitution to make. Just be sure that the recipe is not really high in fat content to begin with, or the texture of the revised recipe may be disappointing. You might begin by substituting applesauce for 1/2 the oil.

Dried Apricot or Date Puree is a yummy and nutritious substitute for eggs and sometimes oil in delicately flavored foods. Place dried apricots in a heat-safe container and pour boiling water over them and allow them to soften, or simmer them in a saucepan with enough water to cover them until they are soft. Drain the water. Puree them in a blender, food processor, or hand-cranked food mill.   **TWO TABLESPOONS OF PUREE=TWO TABLESPOONS OIL OR ONE EGG** Use the drained water in your frozen orange juice or to mash with sweet potatoes.

Whole Wheat Flour is a good substitute to make for white flour whenever possible. The fiber and nutrients in the whole wheat flour are great for the kids! In baked goods, we usually use 1/2 whole wheat flour and 1/2 white flour. The kids rarely know the difference.

If you choose to use whole wheat flours, you need to refrigerate or freeze the mix after 30 days. The oil in the wheat germ is perishable.

Wheat Germ is good for all of us and can be tossed into lots of recipes (cookies, breads, bars, etc.) without even tasting it! Try adding one Tablespoon of raw or toasted wheat germ to each cup of flour or dry ingredients.

Recipe: No-Bake Cookies

Makes:	2 dz.	4 dz.	6 dz.	8 dz.	10 dz.	12 dz.
Ingredients:						
sugar	1 C.	2 C.	3 C.	4 C.	5 C.	6 C.
butter/margarine	1/4 C.	1/2 C.	3/4 C.	1 C.	1 1/4 C.	1 1/2 C.
cocoa powder	3 T.	1/4 C.+2 t.	1/2 C.+1 T.	3/4 C.	3/4 C.+3 T.	1 C.+2 T.
milk	1/4 C.	1/2 C.	3/4 C.	1 C.	1 1/4 C.	1 1/2 C.
peanut butter, creamy	1/3 C.	2/3 C.	1 C.	1 1/3 C.	1 2/3 C.	2 C.
oats, quick or regular	2 C.	4 C.	6 C.	8 C.	10 C.	12 C.
wheat germ (opt.)	1/2 C.	1 C.	1 1/2 C.	2 C.	2 1/2 C.	3 C.
dry milk powder (opt.)	1/2 C.	1 C.	1 1/2 C.	2 C.	2 1/2 C.	3 C.

Containers: rigid freezer containers

Assembly Directions:
In a saucepan, bring the sugar, butter, cocoa powder and milk together to a boil. As soon as it boils, remove it immediately from the heat and stir in the remaining ingredients. While still hot, drop by teaspoons onto waxed paper. Allow to cool and harden.

Freezing Directions:
Label and freeze in rigid containers.

Comments:
This is a healthier version of an age old favorite cookie. The kids will never notice the wheat germ or miss the extra butter.
*Use a cookie scoop for quicker and more uniform cookies.

Recipe: Peanut Butter Balls

Makes:	2 dz.	4 dz.	6 dz.	8 dz.	10 dz.	12 dz.
Ingredients:						
honey or corn syrup	1/3 C.	2/3 C.	1 C.	1 1/3 C.	1 2/3 C.	2 C.
peanut butter, creamy	1/2 C.	1 C.	1 1/2 C.	2 C.	2 1/2 C.	3 C.
dry milk powder	1 C.	2 C.	3 C.	4 C.	5 C.	6 C.
quick oats	1 C.	2 C.	3 C.	4 C.	5 C.	6 C.

Containers: rigid freezer containers or snack size ziptop bags

Assembly Directions:
Mix honey or corn syrup and peanut butter in a bowl. Stir in oats (an electric mixer works well). Stir in just enough milk powder to help the balls hold their shape.   Roll in 24 balls.

Freezing and Serving Directions:
Place on plate or baking sheet and chill to eat now.
To eat later, freeze on tray until firm and place peanut butter balls in rigid freezer containers. Label.
To serve, thaw slightly, but keep chilled. These soften too much at room temperature to be practical for little hands!

Comments:
We haven't tried it yet, but we think these would taste extra yummy with a chocolate coating!

Recipe: Good-for-You Granola

Makes:	12 C.	24 C.	36 C.	48 C.	60 C.	72 C.
Ingredients:						
whole wheat flour	2 C.	4 C.	6 C.	8 C.	10 C.	12 C.
rolled oats	6 C.	12 C.	18 C.	24 C.	30 C.	36 C.
coconut	1 C.	2 C.	3 C.	4 C.	5 C.	6 C.
wheat germ	1 C.	2 C.	3 C.	4 C.	5 C.	6 C.
water	1/2 C.	1 C.	1 1/2 C.	2 C.	2 1/2 C.	3 C.
oil	1 C.	2 C.	3 C.	4 C.	5 C.	6 C.
honey or corn syrup	1 C.	2 C.	3 C.	4 C.	5 C.	6 C.
vanilla extract	2 t.	1 T.+1 t.	2 T.	2 T.+2 t.	3 T.+1 t.	1/4 C.
salt	2 t.	1 T.+1 t.	2 T.	2 T.+2 t.	3 T.+1 t.	1/4 C.
Optional:						
sesame seeds	2 T.	1/4 C.	1/4 C.+2 T.	1/2 C.	1/2 C.+2 T.	3/4 C.
nuts	1/2 C.	1 C.	1 1/2 C.	2 C.	2 1/2 C.	3 C.
dried fruit	1 C.	2 C.	3 C.	4 C.	5 C.	6 C.

Containers: freezer ziptop bags or rigid freezer containers

Assembly Directions:
Combine dry ingredients in a large mixing bowl. Combine remaining ingredients in another bowl. If using nuts and/or seeds, add them to the dry ingredients. Combine the contents of both bowls and mix thoroughly. Spread mixture evenly on two spray-treated or greased large, rimmed cookie sheets. Bake at 250° for 1 hour, stirring twice during baking. Cool and store in airtight containers, or freeze.

Freezing Directions:
Label and freeze in ziptop bags or rigid containers.

Comments:
For out-of-hand snacking, leave the granola in a little larger clumps than you would for eating with a spoon. If you choose to add dried fruit, stir it in after baking and cooling granola thoroughly.

Recipe: Breakfast McBiscuits

Makes:	1 dz.	2 dz.	3 dz.	4 dz.	5 dz.	6 dz.

Ingredients:

Bread:
*homemade biscuits

	1 dz.	2 dz.	3 dz.	4 dz.	5 dz.	6 dz.
*homemade biscuits	12	24	36	48	60	72

OR
purchased refrigerator biscuits
OR
English muffins

Meat:

	1 dz.	2 dz.	3 dz.	4 dz.	5 dz.	6 dz.
Pre-cooked bacon slices	24	48	72	96	120	144
OR						
ham slices	12	24	36	48	60	72
OR						
cooked sausage patties	12	24	36	48	60	72

Eggs:

	1 dz.	2 dz.	3 dz.	4 dz.	5 dz.	6 dz.
scrambled, fried, or poached	1 dz.	2 dz.	3 dz.	4 dz.	5 dz.	6 dz.
Cheese slices	12	24	36	48	60	72

Containers: rigid freezer containers or small ziptop bags

Assembly Directions:
Split muffins or baked biscuits. Top with your choice of topping combinations.
Example: 2 slices of bacon, 1 egg, 1 slice of cheese OR
        1 sausage patty, 1 slice of cheese OR
        1/4 C. scrambled eggs, 1 slice of cheese
Be creative!

Freezing and Serving Directions:
Wrap individually, label, and freeze.
To serve, place thawed, foil-wrapped biscuit in oven and warm at 400° for 20 minutes or unwrap and re-wrap in damp paper towel and microwave a few minutes.

Comments:
Large biscuits are more manageable than small ones. For purchased biscuits, "Grands" brand work well. For homemade biscuits, don't overbake them or they will dry and crumble after reheating.
See our Biscuit recipe in the Master Baking Mix under Snacks/Desserts.

Recipe: Frozen Peanut Butter Bars

Makes:	2 dz.	4 dz.	6 dz.	8 dz.	10 dz.	12 dz.
Ingredients:						
butter/margarine	1 C.	2 C.	3 C.	4 C.	5 C.	6 C.
peanut butter, creamy	2 C.	4 C.	6 C.	8 C.	10 C.	12 C.
*graham cracker crumbs	2 1/2 C.	5 C.	7 1/2 C.	10 C.	12 1/2 C.	15 C.
powdered sugar	1 3/4 C.	3 1/2 C.	5 1/4 C.	7 C.	8 3/4 C.	10 1/2 C.
chocolate chips, semi-sweet or milk chocolate	2 C.	4 C.	6 C.	8 C.	10 C.	12 C.
milk	1/3 C.	2/3 C.	1 C.	1 1/3 C.	1 2/3 C.	2 C.

Containers: rigid freezer containers and freezer ziptop bags

Assembly Directions:
In a large saucepan, melt butter and peanut butter together. Mix well. Remove from heat. Add crumbs and powdered sugar, mixing well. Spread peanut butter mixture in a jelly roll pan (for thinner bars) or 9x13 pan (for thicker bars). Chill. When firm, melt chocolate chips with milk. Spread over chilled peanut butter mixture. Chill again.

Freezing Directions:
Cut into serving size pieces. Wrap individually and freeze in large rigid containers or freezer ziptop bags. Eat straight from the freezer or thaw slightly.

Comments:
Hey, you peanut butter and chocolate lovers! It doesn't get any better than this! If you can keep from eating them, these are great to keep around for company, after school snacking and for a treat after the kids go to bed!

*We have found that we can usually buy the graham cracker crumbs for the same price as the equivalent in graham crackers. Why do the work if you don't have to?

Recipe: Apple Squares

Makes:	24 sqs.	48 sqs.	72 sqs.	96 sqs.	120 sqs.	144 sqs.
Ingredients:						
flour	2 C.	4 C.	6 C.	8 C.	10 C.	12 C.
baking soda	1 t.	2 t.	1 T.	1 T.+1 t.	1 T.+2 t.	2 T.
cinnamon	1 t.	2 t.	1 T.	1 T.+1 t.	1 T.+2 t.	2 T.
salt	1/2 t.	1 t.	1 1/2 t.	2 t.	2 1/2 t.	1 T.
oil	1 C.	2 C.	3 C.	4 C.	5 C.	6 C.
sugar	1 3/4 C.	3 1/2 C.	5 1/4 C.	7 C.	8 3/4 C.	10 1/2 C.
eggs, beaten	4	8	12	16	20	24
vanilla	1 1/2 t.	1 T.	1 T.+1 1/2 t.	2 T.	2 T.+1 1/2 t.	3 T.
apples; unpeeled, chopped	2 C.	4 C.	6 C.	8 C.	10 C.	12 C.
nuts, chopped (opt.)	1/2 C.	1 C.	1 1/2 C.	2 C.	2 1/2 C.	3 C.
Frosting:						
powdered sugar	1 1/2 C.	3 C.	4 1/2 C.	6 C.	7 1/2 C.	9 C.
butter/margarine, melted	2 T.	1/4 C.	1/4 C.+2 T.	1/2 C.	1/2 C.+2 T.	3/4 C.
water	3 T.	1/4 C.+2 T.	1/2 C.+1 T.	3/4 C.	3/4 C.+3 T.	1 C.+2 T.
vanilla	1 t.	2 t.	1 T.	1 T.+1 t.	1 T.+2 t.	2 T.

Containers: rigid freezer containers
Assembly Directions:
Stir together flour, baking soda, cinnamon, and salt. In another bowl, beat together oil, sugar, eggs, and vanilla. Add dry ingredients to liquid, beating well. Stir in apples and nuts (optional). Pour into spray-treated or greased 15 1/2"x10 1/2"x1" cookie sheet or jelly roll pan. Bake at 350° for about 30 minutes or until browned. Cool in pan. Mix all frosting ingredients together until smooth. Drizzle frosting over bars.

Freezing Directions:
Cut into squares. Label and freeze in rigid containers. Use waxed paper between layers.

Comments:
These are great to pull out for drop-in company and taste great at breakfast time, too!
Other fruits such as blueberries, drained pineapple, and sweet cherries may be substituted for the apples.
We have tried this using Egg Beaters to replace the eggs and apricot puree or applesauce to replace all of the oil. Tasted great!
If only a few of you like nuts, sprinkle the nuts over only 1/2 of the pan of batter before baking.

Recipe: Mozzarella Stix

Makes:	32 stix (3 inch)	64 stix	96 stix	128 stix	160 stix	192 stix
Ingredients:						
mozzarella sticks	16	32	48	64	80	96
eggs	2	4	6	8	10	12
water	1 T.	2 T.	3 T.	1/4 C.	1/4 C.+1 T.	1/4 C.+2T.
dry, seasoned bread crumbs (purchased)	1 C.	2 C.	3 C.	4 C.	5 C.	6 C.
paprika	1/2 t.	1 t.	1 1/2 t.	2 t.	2 1/2 t.	1 T.
flour	3 T.	1/4 C.+2 T.	1/2 C.+1 T.	3/4 C.	3/4 C.+3 T.	1 C.+2 T.
On Hand: *Spaghetti Sauce (homemade or purchased)	1 C.	2 C.	3 C.	4 C.	5 C.	6 C.

Containers: Freezer ziptop bags or rigid freezer containers

Assembly Directions:
In a bowl, beat the eggs and water. Place the bread crumbs in a plastic bag. Coat the cheese sticks in flour, then dip in egg mixture and then shake in bread crumb coating.

Freezing and Cooking Directions:
Freeze on cookie sheets. When solid, place in freezer bags or rigid containers.
To serve, place frozen sticks on ungreased baking sheet and bake uncovered at 400° for 6-8 minutes or until thoroughly heated. Allow to set a few minutes before serving. Heat spaghetti sauce for dipping.

Comments:
Our kids really like these! The cheese sticks are very inexpensive at our discount grocery store or you can buy mozzarella cheese and cut it into 3 inch sticks.

*See our Spaghetti Sauce recipe in *Beef Entrees.*

Recipe: Snackin' Mix

Makes:	9 C.	18 C.	27 C.	36 C.	45 C.	54 C.
Ingredients:						
waffle-type cereal	7 C.	14 C.	21 C.	27 C.	35 C.	42 C.
dry roasted, mixed nuts or peanuts	1 C.	2 C.	3 C.	4 C.	5 C.	6 C.
pretzels	1 C.	2 C.	3 C.	4 C.	5 C.	6 C.
butter/margarine, melted	3 T.	6 T.	9 T.	12 T.	15 T.	18 T.
garlic salt	1/4 t.	1/2 t.	3/4 t.	1 t.	1 1/4 t.	1 1/2 t.
onion salt	1/4 t.	1/2 t.	3/4 t.	1 t.	1 1/4 t.	1 1/2 t.
lemon juice	2 t.	1 T.+1 t.	2 T.	2 T.+2 t.	3 T.+1 t.	1/4 C.
Worcestershire sauce	1 T.	2 T.	3 T.	1/4 C.	1/4 C.+1 T.	1/4 C.+2 T.

Containers: rigid freezer containers or snack size ziptop bags

Assembly Directions:
Combine cereal, nuts and pretzels in 9x13 pan or large roasting pan. Set aside. Stir remaining ingredients together Gently stir this mixture into cereal, nuts, and pretzels until evenly coated. Bake at 250° for 45 minutes, stirring every 15 minutes. Spread on paper towels to cool.

Freezing Directions:
Freeze in rigid containers to prevent crushing or in small quantity freezer ziptops for easy snacking. Mix may also be stored at room temperature in an airtight container.

Comments:
The little snack size bags are so easy to grab for lunch boxes, car trips, or a quick outside snack!
Use some of the wheat or multi-bran waffle type cereals for more fiber.
After cooling, add small candy coated chocolates for color (and appeal!).
Our recipe has less oil so it's safer in the mini-van☺
If mix becomes stale, it can be re-crisped for a few minutes in a 350° oven.
Add small lowfat cheese crackers in place of some of the pretzels if you like.

Recipe: Stovetop Cereal Cookies

Makes:	2 dz.	4 dz.	6 dz.	8 dz.	10 dz.	12 dz.
Ingredients:						
brown sugar	1/2 C.	1 C.	1 1/2 C.	2 C.	2 1/2 C.	3 C.
honey or corn syrup	1/4 C.	1/2 C.	3/4 C.	1 C.	1 1/4 C.	1 1/2 C.
vanilla extract	1 t.	2 t.	1 T.	1 T.+1 t.	1 T.+2 t.	2 T.
peanut butter, creamy	3/4 C.	1 1/2 C.	2 1/4 C.	3 C.	3 3/4 C.	4 1/2 C.
ready-to-eat cereal flakes	3 C.	6 C.	9 C.	12 C.	15 C.	18 C.
coconut (optional)	1 C.	2 C.	3 C.	4 C.	5 C.	6 C.

Containers: rigid freezer containers or snack size ziptop bags

Assembly Directions:
Bring brown sugar and honey or corn syrup to a boil in a saucepan. Remove from heat. Stir in vanilla and peanut butter. Mix until smooth. Stir in cereal and coconut (optional). Drop by teaspoons onto waxed paper. Cool until firm.

Freezing and Serving Directions:
Put cookies into rigid freezer containers or snack size ziptop bags and store in refrigerator or freezer.
To serve, thaw slightly, but keep chilled for firmness.

Recipe: Granola Bars

Makes:	16 bars	32 bars	48 bars	64 bars	80 bars	96 bars
Ingredients:						
vegetable oil	1/3 C.	2/3 C.	1 C.	1 1/3 C.	1 2/3 C.	2 C.
brown sugar	3/4 C.	1 1/2 C.	2 1/4 C.	3 C.	3 3/4 C.	4 1/2 C.
honey or corn syrup	2 T.	1/4 C.	1/4 C.+2 T.	1/2 C.	1/2 C.+2 T.	3/4 C.
vanilla	1 t.	2 t.	1 T.	1 T.+1 t.	1 T.+2 t.	2 T.
eggs	1	2	3	4	5	6
whole wheat flour	1 C.	2 C.	3 C.	4 C.	5 C.	6 C.
cinnamon	1 t.	2 t.	1 T.	1 T.+1 t.	1 T.+2 t.	2 T.
baking powder	1/2 t.	1 t.	1 1/2 t.	2 t.	2 1/2 t.	1 T.
salt	1/4 t.	1/2 t.	3/4 t.	1 t.	1 1/4 t.	1 1/2 t.
oats	1 1/2 C.	3 C.	4 1/2 C.	6 C.	7 1/2 C.	9 C.
crisp rice cereal	2 C.	4 C.	6 C.	8 C.	10 C.	12 C.
chopped nuts or sunflower seeds	1 C.	2 C.	3 C.	4 C.	5 C.	6 C.

Optional: raisins, currants, 1 C.   2 C.   3 C.   4 C.   5 C.   6 C.
chocolate chips, peanut butter chips,
carob chips, chopped dried fruit, or a combo
Containers: snack size freezer ziptop bags for individual bars or rigid freezer containers

Assembly Directions:
In a large mixer bowl, combine oil, brown sugar, honey or corn syrup, vanilla, and egg. Add flour, cinnamon, baking powder, and salt. Mix well. With a large spoon, stir in oats, cereal, and nuts, fruits, or baking chips. Spray treat a 9x13 pan. Press the mixture evenly into bottom of pan. For chewy bars, bake at 350° for 20-30 minutes until lightly browned on the edges. For crunchy bars, bake at 300° until the surface is golden brown all over, about 40-50 minutes. Cool completely and cut into 16 bars by slicing through the middle lengthwise, then crosswise 7 times.

Freezing Directions:
Label and freeze in ziptop bags or rigid containers.

Comments:
This version of the supermarket standard is very good and very close to the name brands!
Great for lunches and healthy snacking. Experiment with the options!

Recipe: Oatmeal Cookie Mix

Makes:	32 C. Mix	64 C. Mix	96 C. Mix	128 C. Mix	160 C. Mix	192 C. Mix
Ingredients:						
granulated sugar	3 C.	6 C.	9 C.	12 C.	15 C.	18 C.
brown sugar	3 C.	6 C.	9 C.	12 C.	15 C.	18 C.
flour	6 C.	12 C.	18 C.	24 C.	30 C.	36 C.
salt	1 T.+1 t.	2 T.+2 t.	1/4 C.	1/4 C.+4 t.	1/2 C.	1/2 C.+4t.
baking soda	1 T.+1 t.	2 T.+2 t.	1/4 C.	1/4 C.+4 t.	1/2 C.	1/2 C.+4t.
baking powder	2 t.	1 T.+1 t.	2 T.	2 T.+2 t.	3 T.+1 t.	1/4 C.
shortening	4 C.	8 C.	12 C.	16 C.	20 C.	24 C.
oats (any)	12 C.	24 C.	36 C.	48 C.	60 C.	72 C.
To Make:	**3 dz.**	**6 dz.**	**9 dz.**	**12 dz.**	**15 dz.**	**18 dz.**
eggs	2	4	6	8	10	12
vanilla	2 t.	1 T.+1 t.	2 T.	2 T.+2 t.	3 T.+1 t.	1/4 C.
cookie mix	4 C.	8 C.	12 C.	16 C.	20 C.	24 C.

Containers: 1 or 2 gallon freezer ziptop bags or tightly sealed rigid containers

Assembly Directions:
In large tub, mix first six ingredients with hand mixer or by hand. Cut in shortening with hand mixer. Stir in rolled oats. Place in airtight container if not baking now. Store mix in cool place.

Cooking Directions:
To use mix, combine the mix with the eggs and vanilla. Drop by teaspoonfuls onto baking sheets. Bake at 350° for 10-12 minutes.

Comments:
The cookies may be baked now and frozen, the dough can be frozen in a lump or open frozen in balls for individual cookies, or you can store the dry mix. Nuts, raisins, sunflower seeds, chocolate chips, etc., can be added with the oats or added just before the eggs and vanilla (if storing the dry mix). For all the variations (except chocolate chips) a teaspoon of cinnamon for each batch may be stirred into the eggs.
Having the dry mix made up puts fresh-baked cookies in your families' hands in just a few minutes. It's SO easy!!

30 DAY GOURMET
SNACK/DESSERT/ENTREE

Recipe: Master Baking Mix

Makes:	20-25 C.	40-50 C.	60-75 C.
Ingredients:			
whole wheat pastry flour, or all purpose flour, or a mix	20 C. (5 lbs.)	40 C. (10 lbs.)	60 C. (15 lbs.)
baking powder	3/4 C.	1 1/2 C.	2 1/4 C.
salt	3 T.	1/4 C.+2 T.	1/2 C.+1 T.
cream of tartar	1 T.	2 T.	3 T.
sugar	1/2 C.	1 C.	1 1/2 C.
dry milk powder (optional)	4 C.	8 C.	12 C.

Optional: Add up to 2 C. wheat germ to each recipe. The dry milk powder is optional; it adds protein to the product. You can replace a cup or two of the flour with soy flour for even higher protein counts.

Containers: 1 or 2 gallon ziptop freezer bags, or rigid containers

Assembly Directions:

Sift all the ingredients together at least three times, or stir with a large spoon VERY well. Store in a covered container at room temperature. Label. If it will not be used within a month or two, refrigerate if it contains whole wheat flour or wheat germ.

Muffins: Preheat oven to 425°. In a bowl, stir together:
1 C. milk or buttermilk   1 egg
2 T. sugar   3 T. oil
3 T. applesauce
Add 2 1/2 C. *Master Baking Mix*. Stir just until moistened. Spoon into greased muffin tins or paper liners and bake for 20 minutes. Makes 1 dozen. One C. of dried fruit bits, fresh or frozen blue berries, or nuts may be added to the dry ingredients before adding the liquids.

Quick Bread: Combine ingredients as for muffins. Pour into a greased 5x8 loaf pan and bake at 350° for 40-45 minutes. Great toasted, too! Option: Mash 2 bananas and use only 3/4 C. of milk to make banana bread. A teaspoon of vanilla or coconut extract may be added also!

Biscuits: Preheat oven to 450°. In a bowl, cut 1/4 C. shortening into 1 3/4 C. *Master Baking Mix*. Stir in 1/3 C. of milk all at once. Stir about 20 strokes and knead lightly on a floured board. Roll 1/2" thick and bake on an ungreased baking sheet for 10 minutes.

Drop Biscuits: Mix as for regular biscuits but increase the milk to 3/4 C. Drop by heaping Tablespoons onto greased baking sheets. Grated cheese and garlic powder may be added to make a bread VERY similar to that found in a famous seafood restaurant named for a red crustacean similar to a crab.☺

Pancakes/ Waffles: 2 C. mix added to 1 egg, 1 C. of milk, 1 T. oil, beaten together. Yields 8 - 5" pancakes.

Recipe: Quick Cobbler Mix

Makes:	**1**	**2**	**3**	**4**	**5**	**6**
serves 4-6						

Ingredients:

	1	**2**	**3**	**4**	**5**	**6**
sugar	1 C.	2 C.	3 C.	4 C.	5 C.	6 C.
flour	1 C.	2 C.	3 C.	4 C.	5 C.	6 C.
baking powder	2 t.	1 T.+1 t.	2 T.	2 T.+2 t.	3 T.+1 t.	1/4 C.
salt	1/2 t.	1 t.	1 1/2 t.	2 t.	2 1/2 t.	1 T.

On Hand:

	1	**2**	**3**	**4**	**5**	**6**
milk	1 C.	2 C.	3 C.	4 C.	5 C.	6 C.
fruit; fresh, frozen, or canned	2 C.	4 C.	6 C.	8 C.	10 C.	12 C.

Containers: rigid freezer containers or 1-2 gallon ziptop freezer bags

Assembly Directions:
To Pre-Bake:
Combine sugar, flour, baking powder, and salt in a bowl. Stir in the milk and pour the mixture into a spray-treated 9x9 pan or baking dish. Add the fruit to the top, distributing evenly. Bake at 350° for 30-40 minutes until the top is browned. It looks odd but the crust will rise to the top. Cool.
To Bake on Serving Day:
Mix dry ingredients and store in an airtight container. To bake, measure out 2 C. of the dry mix. Stir in 1 C. milk. Pour the mixture into a spray-treated 9x9 pan or baking dish. Add the fruit to the top, distributing evenly. Bake at 350° for 30-40 minutes until the top is browned. The crust will rise to the top. Serve warm.

Freezing and Serving Directions:
Pre-Baked Cobbler: Thaw completely. Reheat in oven or microwave.

Comments:
We prefer to mix and store the dry ingredients and bake the cobbler fresh. It's really quick as long as you have milk and fruit on hand! The kids can even do this one!
Quick cobbler is fat free (with skim milk) and tastes great for breakfast or dessert.
1 recipe will fit in an 8x8 or 9x9 baking dish.
2 recipes will fit in a 9x13 pan.

30 DAY GOURMET
APPENDIX

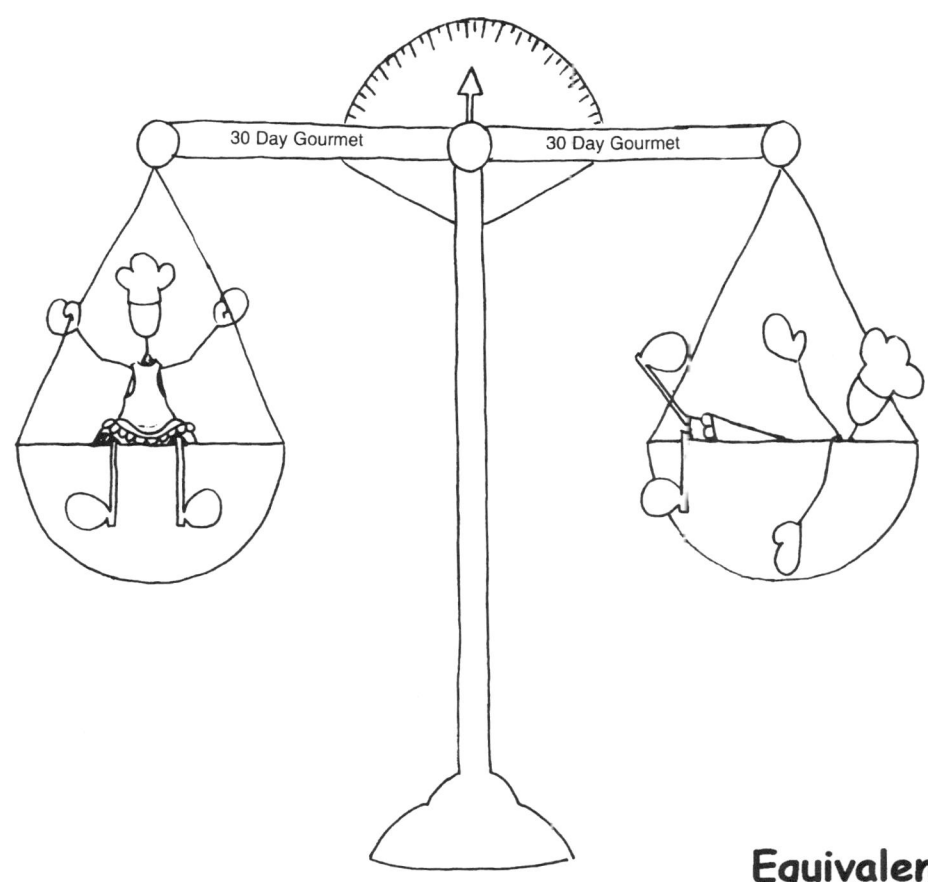

Equivalency Chart
Freezing Time Chart
Blanching Chart
Food Cooperative Information
Web Site Information
Speaking Information
Order Form

EQUIVALENCY CHART

DRY MEASURE

Pinch = a little less than 1/4 teaspoon
3 teaspoons = 1 Tablespoon
2 T. = 1 oz. = 1/8 C.
4 T. = 2 oz. = 1/4 C.
5-1/3 T. = 2.7 oz. = 1/3 C.
8 T. = 4 oz = 1/2 C.
10-2/3 T. = 5.4 oz. = 2/3 C.
12 T. = 6 oz. = 3/4 C.
16 T. = 8 oz. = 1 C.
4 C. = 1 quart
4 quarts = 1 gallon
16 oz. = 1 lb.

LIQUID MEASURE

3 teaspoons = 1 Tablespoon
a dash = a few drops
2 T. = 1 oz.
4 T. - 2 oz. = 1/4 C.
5-1/3 T. = 2.7 oz. = 1/3 C.
8 T. = 4 oz. = 1/2 C.
10-2/3 T. = 6 oz. = 3/4 C.
16 T. = 8 oz. = 1 C.
2 C. = 1 pint = 1/2 quart
4 C. = 2 pints = 1 quart
4 quarts = 16 C. = 1 gallon = 128 oz.

DRY GOODS

Bread Cubes and Crumbs
4 slices of bread = 2 C. fresh soft crumbs
4 slices of bread = 3/4 C. dry crumbs
6 oz. dried bread crumbs = 1 scant cup
16 oz. loaf = 14 C. one inch cubes

Cereal Crumbs
16 oz. corn flake cereal = 5 quarts
2 C. flakes = 3/4 C. crumbs
21 oz. box corn flakes = 7 C. of cereal
15 oz. box puffed rice = 11 C. of cereal
13 oz. box of puffed rice = 6 C. crumbs

Cracker Crumbs
28 soda crackers = 1 C. fine crumbs
16 oz. crackers = 6 C. fine crumbs = 8 C. coarse crumbs
15 square graham crackers = 1 C. crumbs
16 oz. graham crackers = 70 crackers
1 roll of snack crackers = about 1-1/3 C. crumbs
16 oz. of snack crackers = about 5-1/3 C. crumbs
24 round butter crackers = 1 C. fine crumbs
14 oz. box of cracker meal = 3-3/4 C. crumbs

Flours/Meal
1 lb. white flour = 3-1/2 C. or 4 C. sifted
1 lb. whole wheat flour = 3-1/4 C.
1 lb. whole wheat flour, sifted = 3-1/2 C.
1 C. flour = 4 oz.
14 oz. cracker meal = 3-3/4 C.

Butter/Margarine/Shortening
1 T. = 1/2 oz. = 1/8 stick
4 T. = 2 oz. = 1/4 C. = 1/2 stick
8 T. = 4 oz. = 1/2 C. = 1 stick
16 T. = 8 oz. = 1 C. = 2 sticks
32 T. = 16 oz. = 2 C. = 4 sticks = 1 lb.
3 lb. can of shortening = 6 C.

Leavening Agents
16 oz. baking soda = 2- 1/3 C.
16 oz. baking powder = 2-1/3 C.
14 oz. can baking powder = 1-3/4 C.
5-1/2 oz. baking powder = 1 C.
.25 oz. active dry yeast = 1 T.
1 oz. of active dry yeast = 3-1/3 T.
16 oz. of active dry yeast = 3-1/3 C.
.60 oz. compressed yeast = 4 t.

Sweeteners
12 oz. honey = 1 C.
16 oz. honey = 1-1/2 C.
16 oz. corn syrup = 1-1/2 C.
11 oz. molasses = 1 C.
11 oz. maple syrup = 1 C.
16 oz. white sugar = 2-1/3 C.
16 oz. brown sugar = 2-1/4 C. packed
16 oz. powdered sugar = 3-1/2 C.
2/3 C. honey = 1 C. sugar + 1/3 C. water

Cooking Oil   8 oz. = 1 C.

COMMERCIALLY CANNED FOODS

6 oz. can = about 3/4 C.
8 oz. can = about 1 C.
10.5 oz. can = about 1-1/4 C.
14.5 oz. can = about 1-2/3 C.
15.5 oz. can = about 1-3/4 C.
16 oz. can = about 2 C.
20 oz. can = 2-1/2 C.
46 oz. can juice = 5-3/4 C.

COMMERCIALLY FROZEN FOODS

1 oz. frozen vegetables = about 3 T. cooked
4 oz. frozen vegetables = about 3/4 C. cooked
5 oz. frozen vegetables = about 1 C. cooked
10 oz. frozen vegetables = about 2 C. cooked
16 oz. frozen vegetables = about 2-3/4 C. cooked
20 oz. frozen vegetables = about 4 C. cooked

CAN SIZE EQUIVALENTS

Can Size	Measure Amount	Approximate weight
No. 1	1-1/4 C.	10-1/2 oz.
No. 300	1-3/4 C.	15-1/2 oz.
No. 303	2 C.	16 oz.
No. 2	2-1/2 C.	24 oz.

DAIRY PRODUCTS

Shredded and Cubed Cheese
16 oz. = 4 C. cubed or shredded
4 oz. = 1 C. cubed or shredded
Heavy Whipping Cream
1 C. or 8 oz. carton = 2 C. whipped
Parmesan or Romano, grated
6 oz. = 1 C.
16 oz. = 2-2/3 C.
24 oz. = 3 C.
Cottage Cheese
6 oz. = 1 C.
16 oz. = 2-2/3 C.
Sour Cream
16 oz. = 1-3/4 C.
9 oz. = 1 C.
Cream Cheese
8 oz. = 1 C.
3 oz. = 6 T. or about 1/3 C.
1 lb. = 2 C.
Sweetened Condensed Milk
14 oz. can = 1-1/4 C.
Evaporated Milk
14-1/2 oz. can = 1-2/3 C.
6 oz. = 2/3 C.
1 C. = 3 C. whipped volume
Dry Milk Powder
16 oz. = 4 cups dry or 4-5 quarts of liquid
Buttermilk Powder
12 oz. = 3-3/4 quarts of liquid buttermilk
1/4 C. buttermilk powder = 1 C. buttermilk

MEATS

Bacon
8 slices = 1/2 C. cooked and crumbled
16 oz. = about 18 slices
Beef
1 lb. ground = 2-1/2 C. browned
10 lbs. ground = 25 C. browned
1 lb. raw = 3-1/2 C. sliced = 3 C. cubed
Bulk Sausage
1 lb. raw = 2-1/2 C. cooked and crumbled
Chicken, boneless, skinless
7-1/2 lbs. raw = about 25 pieces
1 lb. raw = 2 C. raw ground = 2-2/3 C. raw diced
5 lbs. raw = 12 C. cooked, diced
1 large breast = 3/4 C. cooked, diced
2-1/2 lbs. = 7-8 large pieces
Chicken Thighs
5 lbs. = about 25 pieces
Whole Chicken
2-1/2 lb. chicken = 2-1/2 C. cooked meat off the bone
3-1/2 to 4 lb. chicken = 4 C. cooked meat off the bone
4-1/2 lb. 5 lb. chicken = 6 C. cooked meat off the bone
Crab Meat (real or imitation)
1 lb. cooked and boned meat = 2 cups
Ham
1 lb. whole ham = 2-1/2 C. ground ham
1 lb. whole ham = 3 C. cubed
Turkey Breast
5 lb. raw breast = 10 C. cooked meat off the bone
1 lb. drumstick or thigh = 1-1/8 C. diced cooked meat
Whole Turkey
each lb. of turkey = approx. 1 C. cooked meat
Tuna Fish
6 oz. = 3/4 C. lightly packed

FRUITS

Apples
1 medium = 1 C. chopped
1 lb. = 3 medium
Strawberries/Raspberries
1 pint = 1-3/4 C.
4 oz. = 1 C.
Blueberries
1 lb. = 3 C.

Applesauce
16 oz. = 2 C.
Bananas
1 lb. = 3 med. = 2-1/2 C. diced or 3 C. sliced
1 medium = 1/3 C. mashed
Pineapple
1 lb. = 2-1/2 C. diced

Lemons
1 medium = 3 T. juice
1 medium = 3 T. grated rind
5-8 lemons = 1 C. fresh juice
Oranges
1 = 1/3 C. fresh juice

MISCELLANEOUS

Jams/Jellies/Preserves
6 oz. = 2/3 C.
10 oz. = about 1 C.
16 oz. = 1-1/2 C.
16 oz. = 94 t. = 32 T. = 2 C.

Cocoa Powder
8 oz. = 2 C.
16 oz. = 4 C.
Chocolate Chips
6 oz. = 1 C.
Ketchup
28 oz. = 2-1/2 C.

Ice Cubes
11 cubes = 1 C. liquid
Mayonnaise
1 quart = 32 oz. = 4 C.
Nuts
16 oz. = 4 C.
2 oz. = 1/2 C.

Shredded Coconut
16 oz. = 5 C.
14 oz. = 3-1/4 C.
Peanut Butter
16 oz. = 1-3/4 C.

THICKENING AGENTS
1 T. cornstarch = 2 T. flour = 1 T. arrowroot powder = 1 T. tapioca flour = 1 T. Instant Clear Gel

ONE OUNCE OF WEIGHT TO MEASUREMENT OF HERBS AND SPICES

Allspice, ground	5-1/2 T.	Ginger	6 T.	Black Pepper, ground	1/2 C.
Basil	1/2 C.	Sesame Seed	5 T.	Chili Pepper	1/2 C. + 1-1/2 t.
Bay Leaf, whole	7 T.	Marjoram	1/2 C.	Red Pepper Flakes	1/2 C.+ 1-1/2 t.
Celery Seed	1/4 C.	Mustard, dry,		Poppy Seeds	3-3/4 T.
Cinnamon	5-1/2 T.	ground	6 T. + 1 t.	Rosemary	1/2 C.
Cloves, ground	5-1/2 T.	Nutmeg; ground	5 T.	Sage	1/2 C. + 1-1/2 T.
Cumin Seed	6 T.	Onion Powder	4-1/2 T.	Savory	6-3/4 T.
Curry Powder	5-1/2 T.	Oregano	6 T.	Sesame Seed	5 T.
Dill Weed	6 T.	Paprika	5 T.	Tarragon	6-3/4 T.
Dill Seed	4-1/2 T.	Parsley Flakes	1/2 C. + 1-1/2 t.	Thyme	6-1/3 T.
Garlic Powder	6-1/3 T.			Turmeric	5 T.

VEGETABLES

Carrots
1 lb. = 3 C. shredded= 2 C. diced = 6-8 medium
1 medium carrot = 1/2 C. grated
Cooking Onions
1 lb. = 3 medium = 3 C. sliced or chopped
1 medium onion = 1 C. chopped
1 C. chopped = 1 T. dried, minced
1 C. chopped = 1 teaspoon powdered
1 medium onion = 2/3 C. sautéed
Green Onion
7 medium green onions = 1/2 C. sliced
Green Beans
1 lb. Fresh = 3 C. = 2-1/2 C. cooked
Celery
1 medium bunch = 4 to 5 C. diced
1 medium bunch = 2-1/2 to 3 C. sautéed
1 medium bunch= 3 C. diced = 3-1/2 C. sliced
3 large ribs = about 1-1/2 C. diced
1 Cup diced = 2/3 C. sautéed
1 rib = 1/2 C. sliced or diced
Corn
2-3 fresh ears = 1 C. kernels
Peas
4 oz. = 1 Cup
Potatoes
1 lb. = 3 medium = 2-3/4 C. diced = 3 C. sliced
1 lb. = 2 C. mashed
5 lbs. = 10 C. diced
5 lbs. = 10 C. mashed

Sweet Potatoes
1 lb. = 3 medium = 2-1/2 - 3 diced
Spinach and other greens
1 lb. raw = 10-12 C. torn = 1 C. cooked
10 oz. frozen = 1-1/2 lb. fresh = 1-1/2 C. cooked
Sweet Bell Peppers
1 medium = 1/2 C. finely chopped
1 lb. = 5 medium or 3-1/2 C. diced
Tomatoes
1 lb. = 4 small = 1-1/2 C. cooked
Cabbage
1 lb. = 4 C. - 5 C. shredded
Cauliflower
1 lb. = 1-1/2 C. cooked
Tomato Sauce
8 oz. = 1 scant cup
Garlic
1 medium clove = 1/8 t. garlic powder
1 medium clove = 1/2 t. minced
Water chestnuts
8 oz. sliced = 1 C. drained
8 oz. whole = 1 C. drained
Fresh parsley
1 lb. = 6 C. chopped
Mushrooms
4 oz. fresh = 1 C. whole = 1/2 C. cooked
1 lb. = about 20 large or 40 medium whole
1 lb. = about 4 C. whole = 2 C. cooked
12 oz. = about 3 C. whole

DRY BEANS/GRAINS/PASTA/NUTS

Lentils
6 oz. dry = 1 C.
Kidney Beans
11 oz. dry = 1 C. dry = 3 C. cooked
15 oz. can = 1-3/4 C.
16 oz. dry = 5 C. cooked
Barley
3/4 C. pearl barley = 3 C. cooked
1 C. quick cooking barley = 2-1/2 C. cooked
Long Grain White Rice
16 oz. dry = 2-1/2 C. dry = 10 C. cooked
1 C. dry = 3 C. cooked = 7 oz. dry
Quick Cooking Brown Rice
1 C. dry = 2 C. cooked
12 oz. box = 5-1/3 C. fully cooked, 4-1/2 C. half cooked

White Converted Rice
1 Cup dry = 4 C. cooked
Oatmeal
42 oz. (2 lb. 10 oz. can) = 15 C. cooked oats
1 lb. = 4-5 C. dry
1 C. dry = 3 oz. dry = 1-3/4 C. cooked
Spaghetti
2 oz. = 1 serving = 1/2" diameter dry portion
16 oz. = 4-5 C. dry = 10 C. cooked
Elbow Macaroni
4 oz. = 1 C. dry = 2-1/2 cooked
16 oz. dry = 4 C. dry = 9 C. cooked
Egg Noodles
4 oz. dry = 1 C. dry = 3 C. cooked
16 oz. dry = 4 C. dry = 12 C. cooked
Tiny Pasta (acini pepe, orzo, ditalini, alphabets)
8 oz. = 1-1/3 C.

FREEZING TIME CHART

The following list should give you a good idea of the basics when freezing most ingredients used in **30 DAY GOURMET** cooking. Your local library probably has some very good books that are totally devoted to freezing which are great references. And remember not to skimp while wrapping foods for the freezer. If you use plastic ziptop bags, buy only the ones designed especially for freezing. Freezer wrap works quite well, too and can usually be re-used if you're one of those "saver types"☺.

FOOD	FREEZER LIFE
Baked Goods:	
Bread dough; yeast, unbaked	2 weeks
Baked bread	12 months
Rolls:	
unbaked	2 weeks
1/2 baked	12 months
fully baked	12-15 months
Muffins:	
unbaked	2 weeks
baked	3 months
Waffle/pancake batter	2-4 weeks
Waffles/pancakes, cooked	6 months
Dairy Products	
Butter:	
salted	3 months
unsalted	6 months
Margarine	5 months
Hard cheese	3 months
Cream cheese	3 months
Milk	1 month
Eggs, raw and out of shell	6 months
Produce	
All Vegetables	12 months
Exceptions:	
Asparagus	8-12 months
Onions	6 months
Jerusalem artichokes	3 months
Potatoes	3-6 months
Beets	6 months
Green beans	8-12 months
Leeks	6 months
Winter squash	10 months
Mushrooms	8 months
Corn on the Cob	8-10 months
Herbs	6 months
Vegetable Purees	6-12 months
Prepared Vegetable Dishes	**3 months**
Miscellaneous:	
Pasta, cooked	3-4 months
Pasta, mixed into dishes	3-4 months
Rice, cooked	3-4 months
Rice, mixed into dishes	3-4 months

FOOD	FREEZER LIFE
Beef:	
raw ground beef/stew beef	3-4 months
fresh beef steak	6-12 months
fresh beef roast	6-12 months
fresh beef sausage	3-4 months
smoked beef links or patties	1-2 months
cooked beef dishes	2-3 months
fresh beef in marinade	2-3 months
Pork:	
ground pork	3-4 months
fresh pork sausage	1-2 months
fresh pork chops	4-6 months
fresh pork roast	4-6 months
bacon	1 month
pepperoni	1-2 months
smoked pork links or patties	1-2 months
canned ham	don't freeze
ham, fully cooked	
whole:	1-2 months
half or slices:	1-2 months
pre-stuffed pork chops	don't freeze
cooked pork chops	2-4 months
uncooked casseroles w/ham	1 month
cooked casseroles w/ham	1 month
fresh pork in marinade	2-3 months
Poultry:	
fresh ground turkey	2-3 months
fresh turkey sausage	1-2 months
fresh whole turkey	12 months
chicken or turkey:	
fresh pieces	9 months
cooked pieces	4 months
cooked pieces covered w/broth or gravy	6 months
cooked nuggets	3-4 months
pre-stuffed chicken breasts	don't freeze
cooked poultry dishes	4-6 months
fresh chicken in marinade	2-3 months
Fish:	
fresh pieces	6-12 months
cooked pieces	2-3 months
cooked fish dishes	2-3 months
fish in marinade	2-3 months
Miscellaneous:	
vegetable or meat soups/stews	2-3 months
ground veal and lamb	3-4 months
gravy and meat broths	2-3 months
cooked meat pies	3-4 months
cooked meatloaf	1-3 months

For more extensive information on freezing, please call the USDA Meat and Poultry hotline. You can also request a special packet of free information on safe food handling and freezer power outage problems. 1-800-535-4555

BLANCHING CHART FOR VEGETABLES

Always choose good, quality, fresh vegetables. Clean and trim off inedible parts. Cut to desired size pieces.

MICROWAVE BLANCHING

☑ Choose a rounded microwaveable bowl or container.

☑ Place 1/4 C. of water in the container.

☑ Into the container, place no more than 4 C. of leafy vegetables (like spinach) or 2 C. of other vegetables.

☑ Cover the container with microwaveable plastic wrap.

☑ Make sure that if you have a turntable, it can move freely.

☑ Microwave according to the chart below on highest power setting.

☑ After blanching, spread vegetables out in a single layer on a tray or baking sheet and cool 5 minutes. They are now suitable for freezing by themselves, or in a freezer recipe.

STOVE TOP STEAMING

☑ Prepare vegetable as above.

☑ Use a pan that a wire mesh basket or steamer basket will fit into (at least 8 qt. size).

☑ Bring 1 inch of water to a rolling boil in the pan.

☑ Place no more than 1 pound of vegetables in the basket and place over the steaming water.

☑ Time according to the chart below.

☑ Remove the basket of vegetables from the pot and plunge into cold or ice water, or run cold water over them. This stops the cooking action.

☑ Drain well. The vegetables are now ready for freezing or using in a freezer recipe.

BOILING WATER BLANCHING

☑ Clean and prepare vegetables as above.

☑ In a large pot, bring at least 1 gallon of water for every pound of vegetables to a rolling boil.

☑ Plunge the vegetables in the water 1 pound at a time.

☑ When the water begins to boil again, start timing according to the chart below.

☑ At the end of the blanching time, remove vegetables from the water with a slotted spoon, steamer basket, or strainer with a handle.

☑ Cool hot vegetables as for range top steaming. The vegetables are now ready for use in the freezer.

BLANCHING CHART

VEGETABLE	MICRO-STEAM	RANGE TOP STEAM	BOILING WATER
beets			30-45 min.
broccoli	5 min.	3-5 min.	2-4 min.
Brussels sprouts	4 min.	6 min.	4 min.
cabbage wedges	3 min.	4 min.	3 min.
carrots	2-5 min.	4-5 min.	2-5 min.
cauliflower	5 min.	5 min.	3 min.
celery	3 min.	4 min.	3 min.
corn on the cob			6-8 min.
corn cut from cob	4 min.	6 min.	4 min.
green beans	3 min.	4 min.	3 min.
peas, all types	4 min.	6 min.	4 min.
potatoes:cubed,sliced,or shredded	10 min.	12 min.	10 min.
spinach/other greens		3 min.	2 min.
sweet potatoes	Any method will work. Cook until soft.		
zucchini, cubed	2-3 min.	2-3 min.	2-3 min.

NO BLANCHING NEEDED FOR: mushrooms, onions, peppers, tomatoes, shredded zucchini

Note: If you live at a high altitude, add 30 seconds to the blanching time for every 1000 feet above sea level.

FOOD COOPERATIVE INFORMATION

There are some great reasons to belong to a food buying club. A few that we've found are:

☑ Access to hundreds of healthy foods. Supermarkets who carry healthy foods rarely offer very many choices or low prices. Food co-ops have both!
☑ Large quantities for bulk rates. The food will be cheaper because many families are buying together and guaranteeing a minimum dollar amount purchase. Co-op members often split cases, 50 lb. bags of flour, etc.
☑ Save lots of time by shopping less frequently.

How to find a food cooperative in your area?

☑ Ask around. For one week, ask everyone you see, "Do you know anyone who is in a food co-op?" Then follow up on your leads.
☑ Call one of these bulk distributors and ask them where the closest local food buying club is.

Associated Buyers	**Somersworth, VT**	**802-257-5656**
Blooming Prairie Warehouse	**Iowa City, IA**	**319-337-6448**
Clear Eye Natural Foods	**Carusa, NY**	**315-365-3949**
E & S Sales	**1235 N. State Rd. 5, Shipshewana, IN 46565**	**mail order only**
Federation of Ohio River Co-ops	**Columbus, OH**	**614-861-2446**
Frontier Herbs	**Norway, IA**	**319-227-7991**
New England Buying Club	**Battleboro, VT**	**802-257-5856**
North Farm Cooperative	**Madison, WI**	**1-800-236-5880**
Mountain People's Northwest	**Seattle, WA**	**206-467-7190**
Ozark Co-op Warehouse	**Fayetteville, AR**	**501-521-4920**
Rainbow Distributing	**Chicago, IL**	**773-929-7629**
Something Better Natural Foods	**Battle Creek, MI**	**616-965-1199**
Tuscon Cooperative Warehouse	**Tuscon, AZ**	**520-884-9951**
Mountain People's Warehouse	**Los Angeles, CA**	**1-800-679-6733**

We live in the Indianapolis area and personally know of at least 10 food buying clubs in our area. We regularly order from *Something Better Natural Foods, Federation of Ohio River Co-ops (FORC), and E & S Sales*. A few of the products we most commonly buy are:

Dried apricots	$2.49 lb.	Whole wheat lasagna	.94 lb.
Sunflower seeds	.89 lb.	Whole wheat spaghetti	.81 lb.
Quick brown rice	$1.09 lb.	Texturized vegetable protein	.89 lb.
Rolled oats	.52 lb.	Honey	.92 lb.
Chicken broth powder	$5.32 lb.	Raw wheat germ	.70 lb.
Canola oil	$10.19 gallon	Beef broth powder	$4.68 lb.
Chex cereal	$3.90/2 lbs.	Spanish peanuts	$1.29 lb

We're on the Web....

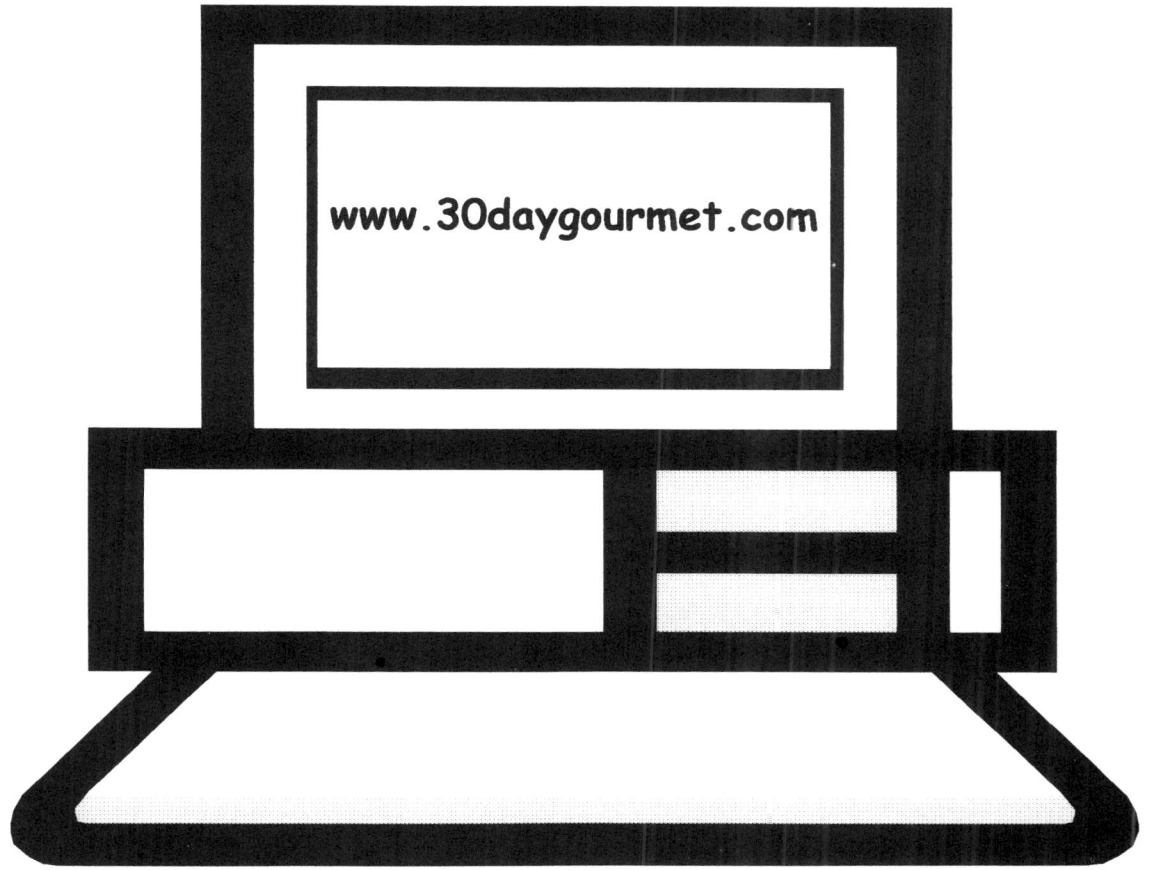

www.30daygourmet.com

- ✦ **50 More Recipes**
  - User name: recipes
  - Password: macaroni
- ✦ **Message Boards**
- ✦ **Chat Room**
- ✦ **E-mail the Authors**
- ✦ **Photo Album**
- ✦ **Speaking Schedule**

30 DAY GOURMET

Learn to cook less, eat more and have fun doing it!!

Seminar will cover:
* What is a 30 Day Gourmet?
* Rewards of Cooking BIG!
* The Buddy System
* Slide Show Featuring:
    Shopping Strategies
    Assembly Methods
    Packaging for the Freezer
    Hints & Tips

Nanci Slagle & Tara Wohlenhaus

Schedule 30 Day Gourmet
to entertain and inform your group of busy cooks

- ❖ Businesses
- ❖ Churches
- ❖ Libraries

- ❖ Conventions
- ❖ Women's Retreats
- ❖ Television & Radio

I saw your "act" last week - you were wonderful! How you combined hilariously funny and informative - WOW!
                                      Linda from Iowa

*An enthusiastic thumbs up on the **30 Day Gourmet** seminar. Thanks for all the good wisdom you are passing along! You've made our lives so much simpler already!*
                                    Dawn and Denise from Kansas

Our current speaking schedule along with terms and prices is available on our web site. Call our office or e-mail us to schedule a **30 Day Gourmet** Seminar.

    Phone: 1-800-9-MANUAL   **e-mail: office@30daygourmet.com**

30 DAY GOURMET ORDER FORM

Customer Name: _____ Date: _____

Address: _____

City: _____ State: _____ Zip Code: _____

Telephone Number: (_____) _____ - _____ e-mail address: _____
(if applicable)

30 DAY GOURMET COOKING MANUAL $25.00

Our comprehensive system for assembling and freezing 4-6 weeks' worth of tasty, nutritious entrees, side dishes and snacks in an easy-to-follow format. Includes:

- Time Saving Worksheets
- Step-By-Step Instructions
- 60+ Delicious Recipes
- Cooking Tips & Practical Money-Saving Advice
- 100+ Equivalents
- Master Mixes
- 20+ Easy Sauces & Marinades
- Indispensable Tally Sheet
- Nutritious Snacks

30 DAY GOURMET COOKING APRONS $15.00

- Style 1: "30 DAY GOURMET" logo
- Style 2: "Great Cooks Do It Once-A-Month" with 30 Day Gourmet logo

Color: Royal Blue with dark yellow print   *Adjustable Neck Strap*
Material: Durable 50% poly/50% cotton, washable   *Size: 30" X 36" (knee length)*

30 DAY GOURMET HOLIDAY COOKING BOOKLET $8.00

Our system for assembling and freezing your entire holiday meal. No more all night cooking. Make dinner when you have the time! Out traditional feasts serve 6 – 36 guests without the traditional hassle. Includes:

- Easy Step-By-Step Instructions
- Freezing and Cooking Tips
- Low-Fat Alternatives
- 26 Delicious recipes multiplied to feed gatherings from 6 – 36 guests

QTY	DESCRIPTION	PRICE	TOTAL
	30 DAY GOURMET COOKING MANUAL ($5.00 S/H)	$25.00	
	ADDITIONAL COOKING MANUAL ($2.50 each add'l manual	$22.00	
	30 DAY GOURMET HOLIDAY COOKING BOOK ($2.00 S/H)	$8.00	
	30 DAY GOURMET COOKING APRON ($3.00 S/H)	$15.00	
	GREAT COOKS DO IT ONCE-A-MONTH APRON ($3.00 S/H)	$15.00	

Please call with shipping questions.

Prices effective through 12/98

SUB TOTAL	
IN. RESIDENTS ADD 5% SALES TAX	
SHIPPING/HANDLING (See Above)	
TOTAL	

Payment

Method: ☐ **Master Card** ☐**Visa** ☐**Discover** ☐**AmEx** ☐ **Personal Check** ☐**M.O.**
(Check One)

Card Number: ☐☐☐☐ – ☐☐☐☐ – ☐☐☐☐ – ☐☐☐☐

Expiration Date: __ __ / __ __ **Signature:** _____

30 DAY GOURMET
P.O. Box 272
Brownsburg, IN 46112
Toll-free: 1-800-9-MANUAL or 317/852-8499
Website: www.30daygourmet.com

30 DAY GOURMET ORDER FORM

Customer Name: _____ Date: _____

Address: _____

City: _____ State: _____ Zip Code: _____

Telephone Number: (_____) _____ - _____ e-mail address:_____
(if applicable)

30 DAY GOURMET COOKING MANUAL $25.00

Our comprehensive system for assembling and freezing 4-6 weeks' worth of tasty, nutritious entrees, side dishes and snacks in an easy-to-follow format. Includes:

- ❖ Time Saving Worksheets
- ❖ Step-By-Step Instructions
- ❖ 60+ Delicious Recipes
- ❖ Cooking Tips & Practical Money-Saving Advice
- ❖ 100+ Equivalents
- ❖ Master Mixes
- ❖ 20+ Easy Sauces & Marinades
- ❖ Indispensable Tally Sheet
- ❖ Nutritious Snacks

30 DAY GOURMET COOKING APRONS $15.00
- ❖ Style 1: "30 DAY GOURMET" logo
- ❖ Style 2: "Great Cooks Do It Once-A-Month" with 30 Day Gourmet logo

Color: Royal Blue with dark yellow print   *Adjustable Neck Strap*
Material: Durable 50% poly/50% cotton, washable   *Size: 30" X 36" (knee length)*

30 DAY GOURMET HOLIDAY COOKING BOOKLET $8.00

Our system for assembling and freezing your entire holiday meal. No more all night cooking. Make dinner when you have the time! Out traditional feasts serve 6 – 36 guests without the traditional hassle. Includes:
- ❖ Easy Step-By-Step Instructions
- ❖ Freezing and Cooking Tips
- ❖ Low-Fat Alternatives
- ❖ 26 Delicious recipes multiplied to feed gatherings from 6 – 36 guests

QTY	DESCRIPTION	PRICE	TOTAL
	30 DAY GOURMET COOKING MANUAL ($5.00 S/H)	$25.00	
	ADDITIONAL COOKING MANUAL ($2.50 each add'l manual	$22.00	
	30 DAY GOURMET HOLIDAY COOKING BOOK ($2.00 S/H)	$8.00	
	30 DAY GOURMET COOKING APRON ($3.00 S/H)	$15.00	
	GREAT COOKS DO IT ONCE-A-MONTH APRON ($3.00 S/H)	$15.00	

Please call with shipping questions.

Prices effective through 12/98

SUB TOTAL	
IN. RESIDENTS ADD 5% SALES TAX	
SHIPPING/HANDLING (See Above)	
TOTAL	

Payment Method: ☐ **Master Card** ☐**Visa**   ☐**Discover** ☐**AmEx** ☐ **Personal Check** ☐**M.O.**
(Check One)

Card Number: ☐☐☐☐ – ☐☐☐☐ – ☐☐☐☐ – ☐☐☐☐

Expiration Date: __ __/ __ __   **Signature:** _____

30 DAY GOURMET
P.O. Box 272
Brownsburg, IN 46112
Toll-free: 1-800-9-MANUAL or 317/852-3499
Website: www.30daygourmet.com